Modellwerkstatt
Model Workshop

Bauprozess
im Entwurfsstudio
Building as a
Common Process

Carmen Rist-Stadelmann
Urs Meister
(Hg./eds.)

Universität Liechtenstein
University of Liechtenstein

 PARK BOOKS

Bretter und Balken 6
Boards and Beams 11

Hands-on als didaktische
Methode 21
Hands-on Didactics 27

Materialbewusstsein
und Tektonik 36
Material Consciousness
and Tectonics 42

Handwerk als kollektiver
Prozess 51
Craft as Collective Process 57

Methoden des Bauens 66
Methods of Building 73

Inhalt Contents

Experimentelle Prototypen 79
Experimental Prototypes 79

Die Urhütte 98
The Primitive Hut 104

Eine Werkstatt für die Universität 116
A Workshop for the University 120

Factbox 133
Fact Box 137

Quellenangaben 140
List of References 141

Impressum 142
Imprint 142

Bretter und Balken
Boards and Beams

Carmen Rist-Stadelmann
Urs Meister

Die Modellwerkstatt der Universität Liechtenstein ist ein zentraler Raum für die Architekturausbildung und wurde bereits 2007 als ein Laborprojekt im Selbstbau mit Studierenden konzipiert. Eine parametrisch entworfene und maschinell geschnittene Kartonwabenstruktur war passgenau mit einem eng anliegenden Kleid aus Lastwagenplanen eingedeckt. Der *bubble*, als Provisorium errichtet, wies aber nach einigen Jahren starke Gebrauchsspuren und Feuchtigkeitsprobleme auf. Im Oktober 2016 stellte die Universität ein Budget bereit und gab dem Institut für Architektur und Raumentwicklung damit die Möglichkeit, die Modellwerkstatt neu als experimentellen Holzbau zu denken, zu planen und schliesslich selbst zu bauen.

Ein experimenteller Prozess

Als erstes verknüpften wir die Bauaufgabe mit einem Workshop im Rahmen des Erasmus+-Programmes „Crafting the façade", das von der Universität Liechtenstein koordiniert und gemeinsam mit der Academie van Bouwkunst, Amsterdam, und der Mackintosh School of Architecture, Glasgow, getragen wurde.

Innerhalb von drei Tagen experimentierten die Studierenden mit Holzbrettern und -balken und entwickelten daraus Konzepte für das Tragwerk der Modellwerkstatt, die im Massstab 1:1 hinter der Universität aufgebaut wurden. Diese Prototypen stellten die Ausgangslage für die Weiterentwicklung in einem experimentellen Prozess dar, in dem die Autorenschaft geteilt wurde. Zwei Entwurfsstudios des Bachelorstudiums nahmen die Strukturkonzepte auf und führten sie bis zur Umsetzung des gesamten Gebäudes weiter. Von den acht zur Auswahl stehenden Tragstrukturen wurden vier Varianten konstruktiv überprüft, verfeinert und als Prototypen im Massstab 1:1 gebaut. In einem Auswahlverfahren wurde die innovativste und gleichzeitig auch realisierbare Tragstruktur gekürt. Innerhalb einer Seminarwoche stellten die Studierenden in der Werkstatt des Zimmereibetriebs Frommelt Holzbau, Schaan, die Rohbauelemente her und richteten hinter der Universität den Holzbau auf den vom Baumeister vorbereiteten Fundamenten auf.

Gespannte Bögen

Die Tragstruktur der Werkstatt besteht aus gebogenen Brettern, welche bogenförmig ausgelegt und, auf einer fix montierten Lehre um die halbe Breite versetzt, wellenförmig unterspannt wurden. Die Gegenspannung garantiert trotz der Feinheit der Bretter die statische Höhe. Um die Biegung zu ermöglichen, war es notwendig, die Bretter je nach Radius auf die geeignete Dicke zu hobeln. Die Optimierung des einzelnen Tragelements machte eine grosse Anzahl von Versuchen und Bruchtests notwendig. Die Verbindungen zwischen Ober- und Untergurt wurden mit verleimten Hartholzkeilen und wenigen sichtbaren Schrauben gewährleistet. So wurden in der Werkhalle Dachelemente von einem Meter Breite hergestellt, die in sich stabil und trotzdem leicht in der Handhabung sind. Das Aufrichten wurde zu einer leichten Aufgabe, die von Hand und nur mithilfe von einigen Böcken möglich war. Eine darüberliegende Bretterlage stabilisiert die Konstruktion in Längsrichtung und bildet die Unterlage für eine moderate Dämmebene, die Hinterlüftung und schliesslich die Wetterhaut aus Lärchenschindeln. Die zusammengebaute, additiv organisierte Struktur ist von grosser Filigranität und demonstriert die Spannung, welche dem Holz immanent ist, auf elegante Weise.

Perspektivenwechsel

Im Entwurf und Bau der Modellwerkstatt entstand im Wechsel der Massstäbe eine grosse Spannung, die über das klassische, lineare Entwickeln vom Grossen zum Kleinen hinausreicht. Das stetige Schärfen und Schleifen in einem Prozess mit wechselnden Perspektiven und unterschiedlichen Distanzen zum Gestalteten erhöhte nicht nur die konstruktive Präzision, sondern auch die Qualität des Entworfenen insgesamt. Entsprechend dem Fortschritt im Bauprozess lösten die Studierenden unterschiedliche Bauaufgaben, um diese anschliessend unmittelbar bauen zu können. Die dabei gemachten Erfahrungen im realen Massstab und im direkten Kontakt mit den Materialien beim Bohren, Sägen, Hobeln und Schindeln halfen, die konstruktiven Zusammenhänge nachhaltig nachzuvollziehen. Diese Unmittelbarkeit der Erfahrungen und der Einbezug von raschen Massstabswechseln bildet in einem weiteren Sinne das direkte didaktische Konzept der Architekturausbildung im Bereich Craft an unserem Institut ab. Das Hin und Zurück von der Ebene des Details und der haptischen Realität zum Ganzen des Bauwerks und zu seinem Ausdruck in einer entwerferischen Reflexion scheint uns entscheidend für das Erreichen einer innovativen Architektur. Zwar hat das computerdominierte Entwerfen das Entwickeln aus der Logik der Materialien seit Ende des 20. Jahrhunderts zunehmend aus der Architekturausbildung vertrieben. Mittlerweile gehören aber das hybride Entwerfen und das handwerkliche Herstellen wieder als starke Pfeiler in die Curricula der meisten europäischen Architekturschulen.

Handwerk und kulturelle Identität

Im Bau der Modellbauwerkstatt wurde unter dem Begriff Handwerk nicht nur das eigentliche Handanlegen, sondern vielmehr auch die Beschäftigung mit der Logik des Fügens der Materialien hin zu einem charakteristischen Ausdruck des Gebauten verstanden. Die Tatsache, dass der Bau von mehrheitlich handwerklich unerfahrenen Studierenden ohne Vorwissen realisiert wurde, spielte bei der Entwicklung eine wichtige Rolle. Fachliche Unterstützung erhielten wir von Christoph Frommelt und den Handwerkern der Zimmerei Frommelt, die mit Ruhe und Weitblick den Studierenden zur Seite standen. Neben dem Entstehungsprozess spielte schliesslich auch das gebaute Resultat und dessen handwerklicher Ausdruck eine entscheidende Rolle — Prozess und Produkt sehen wir als gleichwertige Ziele in der Realisierung der neuen Modellwerkstatt.

Holz ist eine lokale Ressource und ein wichtiger kultureller Identitätsträger. Das Zusammenspiel von Praxis und Lehre erlaubt uns zum einen, das Wissen des regionalen, traditionell verankerten Handwerks in der Architekturausbildung weiterzugeben und soziale, baukulturelle und gesellschaftlichen Aspekte in die Lehre zu integrieren. Zum anderen entsteht durch die aktive Integration in den Entwurfs- und Bauprozess eine direkte Identifikation der Studierenden mit dem gebauten Objekt. Diesen sozialen Aspekt, das gemeinsame Schaffen der neuen Räumlichkeiten in Teamarbeit und die dabei gewonnenen Erfahrungen, bringen die Studierenden in weiteren Schritten in ihren Entwürfen durch das Verständnis des Materials wieder zum Ausdruck — in Zeiten der Globalisierung ein nicht zu unterschätzender Aspekt für die Stärkung der kulturellen Identität der Region und des Handwerks in der Architekturausbildung.

The University of Liechtenstein's model workshop is a key space for architectural education and had been conceived back in 2007 as a self-build lab project conducted with students. A parametrically designed and machine-cut structure of honeycomb cardboard was covered with a precisely tailored, closely fitting gown of truck tarpaulins. But the bubble, erected as a temporary solution, exhibited signs of heavy wear and problems with moisture after a few years. In October 2016, the university allocated a budget that gave the Institute of Architecture and Planning the opportunity to rethink the model workshop as an experimental timber structure, to design it and to ultimately build it themselves.

An experimental process

The starting point for the design process was a five-day workshop, held as part of the Erasmus+ programme 'Crafting the Façade', that was coordinated by the University of Liechtenstein and jointly conducted over a period of three years with the Academie van Bouwkunst in Amsterdam and the Mackintosh School of Architecture.

Within a three-day period, the students experimented with wooden boards and beams and used them to develop concepts for the model-making workshop's load-bearing structure, which were built behind the university, on a scale of 1:1. These prototypes constituted the starting point for continued development in an experimental process in which authorship was shared. Two design studios in the Bachelor's degree programme took the structural concepts and carried them forward to successful realisation of the whole building. Of the eight load-bearing structures available to choose from, four variants were structurally vetted, refined and built as prototypes at full scale. A selection process was used to choose the most innovative and yet feasible load-bearing structure. Within one seminar week, the students fabricated the structural elements in the workshop of Frommelt Holzbau, a carpentry contractor in Schaan, and erected the timber construction behind the university on foundations prepared by the master builder.

Tensioned arches

The workshop's load-bearing structure consists of curved boards that were laid out in an arch shape on a fixed jig and then trussed together in an undulating pattern, offset by half their width. The counter-tension ensures sufficient static height despite the fineness of the boards. To achieve the curvature, it was necessary to plane the boards to the suitable thickness depending on the radius. For optimisation of the individual load-bearing element, a large number of trials and fracture tests were necessary. The connections between the upper and lower chords were secured with glued hardwood wedges and a few visible screws. In this way, roof elements of one-meter width, which are stable in themselves and yet convenient to handle, were produced on the shop floor. Lifting the elements up into position became an easy task that could be done by hand and with the aid of just a few trestles. A layer of boards above stabilises the structure longitudinally and forms the substrate for a moderate insulation layer, ventilation space and, lastly, the weather barrier made of larch shingles. The assembled, additively arranged structure is extremely delicate and elegantly demonstrates the internal stresses intrinsic to the wood.

Change of perspective

In designing and building the model workshop, the variation of scales engendered great potential that goes beyond that of classic linear development from the large to the small. The constant sharpening and honing in a process with changing perspectives and varied distances to that which is being designed increased not only the constructive precision, but also the quality of the design as a whole. As the process of building progressed, the students solved different construction tasks in order to subsequently be in a position to build them directly. The experience gained on a real scale and in direct contact with the materials while drilling, sawing, planing and shingling helped them to deeply and lastingly comprehend the constructional contexts. In a broader sense, this immediacy of experience and the inclusion of rapid changes of scale illustrate the direct didactic concept of architectural education at our institute in respect to craft. The back and forth in reflection on the design—from the level of details and tangible reality to the expression of the whole of the building—seems to us to be crucial for attaining innovative architecture. Although computer-dominated design has, since the end of the 20th century, increasingly driven the concept of developing from the logic of materials out of architectural education, hybrid design and craft-based production are once again a strong pillar in the curricula of most European architecture schools.

Craft and cultural identity

In the construction of the modelmaking workshop, the concept of craft was understood not only in terms of the actual work done by hand, but rather also as engaging with the logic of joining the materials to achieve a characteristic expression of the built. The fact that the construction work was mostly done by students with no experience in skilled trades and no prior relevant knowledge played an important role in the development. We received expert technical support from Christoph Frommelt and the craftspeople from the Frommelt carpentry shop, who assisted the students with composure and foresight. In addition to the origination process, the built result and its handcrafted expression ultimately also played a decisive role—we see process and product as equally important goals in the realisation of the new model workshop.

Wood is a local resource and an important conveyor of cultural identity. The interplay of practice and teaching allows us to pass on the knowledge of the region's traditionally anchored crafts in architectural education and to integrate social, societal and building cultural aspects into the instruction. Moreover, their active integration into the design and construction process engenders direct identification with the built object amongst the students. This social aspect, the collective creation of the new facilities through teamwork and the experiences gained in the process are expressed by the students again in subsequent steps in their designs through an understanding of the material—and in times of globalisation, this aspect should not be underestimated for strengthening both the region's cultural identity and skilled crafts in architectural education.

Erasmus+ Workshop Crafting Wood

Erasmus+ Workshop Crafting Wood

Man erhält ein ganz anderes Gefühl, wenn die Aktivität zuerst erlebt wird und erst danach im Kopf entsteht. Das damit verbundene genaue Beobachten, wie die Konstruktion bis ins Detail ausgeführt wird, erweiterte das eigene Wissen. Ich glaube, dass dies sehr wertvoll für das eigene Entwerfen und Überlegen ist.

Joanne Tschenett
MSc Studierende

You get a completely different feeling when you experience the activity first and it only emerges in your mind afterwards. Being able to closely observe in detail how the construction work is carried out expanded one's own knowledge. I think this is very valuable for one's own designing and thinking.

Joanne Tschenett
MSc student

Hands-on als didaktische Methode
Hands-on Didactics

Carmen Rist-Stadelmann

One must learn by doing the thing; for though you think you know it, you have no certainty, until you try.

Sophokles[1]

1938 veröffentlichte der amerikanische Psychologe und Erziehungswissenschaftler John Dewey sein pädagogisch-philosophisches Buch „Experience and Education". Darin misst er Experimenten, die zur Vermittlung und Erarbeitung von Lerninhalten eingesetzt werden, eine grosse Bedeutung zu. In Deweys Vorstellung hat die Erziehung primär die Aufgabe, die eigenen Fähigkeiten für das Neue zu fördern und dabei ein Bewusstsein für das Gemeinsame zu entwickeln. Neben dem Lernen der Fachkompetenzen integrieren Experimente in seinem Verständnis auch die ebenso wichtigen Sozial- und Beziehungskompetenzen. Sie beinhalten Methoden, um das Lernen effektiv zu steuern und dieses zusammen mit dem fachlichen Lernen zu vermitteln.[2] Zudem müssen für ihn Experimente immer in das Leben von Individuum und Gesellschaft, in ein reales Umfeld integriert sein.[3]

Neben dem Experiment fokussiert Dewey in seiner Lerntheorie auf Lernimpulse, die ein positives Lernen auslösen und ermöglichen. Stimulierende Lernprozesse verändern laut Dewey den Lernprozess, wecken Neugierde und erzeugen den Wunsch nach konkreten Erfahrungen in Form von zielgerichtetem Handeln.[4] Impulse für ein eigenständiges Urteilsvermögen entstehen für ihn in der Lenkung der natürlichen Handlungsimpulse der Lernenden durch „stop and think", dem Austausch der Gedanken in Kombination der Augen und Hände. Denken ist immer ein nachträgliches Verfahren, um über etwas nachzudenken. Selbstkontrolle ermöglicht laut Dewey die Entwicklung eines eigenen Urteilsvermögens und sollte deshalb verstärkt gelehrt werden.[5]

Für Dewey ist der Unterricht kein fertiges Produkt, sondern bereitet den Lernenden im Idealfall für ein lebenslanges Lernen vor.[6] Der Unterricht muss flexibel sein, um ein eigenes Lernen zu ermöglichen und ein eigenes Forschen zu erlauben.[7] Seine Lerntheorien besitzen bis heute Gültigkeit und waren ihrer damaligen Zeit weit voraus. Besonders seine Methoden des Experiments, Laboratory Studies und Field Projects fanden Zuspruch und finden sich bis heute in Curricula quer durch die unterschiedlichsten Ausbildungsdisziplinen wieder.[8]

Aktionsforschung

In der Haltung, dass Ausbildung eine demokratische Beteiligung der Involvierten und eine soziale Gerechtigkeit beinhalten muss, stimmen Kurt Lewin und John Dewey überein.[9] Während Dewey seine Lernmethoden mehr als Impulse verstand, fokussiert Lewin seine Arbeit auf Prozesse und entwickelte daraus neue wissenschaftliche Methoden. Für Lewin war die Integration von Praxis und Theorie von grosser Bedeutung, was sich in seinen umfangreichen Beratungs- und Forschungstätigkeiten in der amerikanischen Industrie widerspiegelt.[10]

Als besondere Form der wissenschaftlichen Untersuchung realisierte Lewin in den 1940er-Jahren ein Verfahren mit dem Ziel, Kenntnisse über ein soziales System zu erlangen und dieses dabei gleichzeitig beeinflussen zu können.[11] Dieses Verfahren beschreibt er in seinem 1946 publizierten Artikel „Aktionsforschung und Minoritätenprobleme"[12] und definiert darin den Prozess von einer Idee zu einem Ziel in einer Abfolge von Schritten. Der erste Schritt beinhaltet das Abwägen der Idee im Verhältnis zu den zur Verfügung stehenden Mitteln, um das Ziel zu erreichen. Es impliziert das Sammeln von Daten und das Beobachten im Hier und Jetzt. Die anschliessende Entwicklung eines Gesamtplanes zeigt, wie das Ziel zu erreichen ist. Als nächster Schritt erfolgt die Evaluation der ersten Handlungsschritte und die Entscheidung, ob eventuelle Abänderungen bei der Handlung nötig sind. Anschliessend wird die Handlung wieder evaluiert und darauf aufbauend die weitere Vorgehensweise entschieden.[13] Lewin misst in diesem ganzen Prozess dem Feedback eine grosse Bedeutung bei, um die dabei gemachten abstrakten und konkreten Erfahrungen in der Forschungsgruppe zu teilen und überprüfen zu können. Diesen für die Aktionsforschung typischen Ablauf von Planung, Aktivität, Beobachtung und Reflektion impliziert seine schrittweise Reflektion der wissenschaftlichen Untersuchung bereits in ihrer Vorgangsweise. Lewin bemerkt dazu: *Wenn wir nicht beurteilen können, ob eine Handlung uns vorangebracht oder zurückgeworfen hat, wenn uns die Kriterien für eine Bewertung des Verhältnisses zwischen Aufwand und Ertrag fehlen, dann hindert uns nichts an einer falschen Schlussfolgerung.*[14]

Assimilation und Akkommodation

Für den Schweizer Psychologen und genetischen Epistemologen Jean Piaget entsteht ein Lernprozess, wie bei Kurt Lewin und John Dewey, durch das Zusammenspiel von Umgebung und Individuum.[15] Piaget erklärt dieses Zusammenspiel mit den Begriffen Assimilation und Akkommodation, der gegenseitigen Interaktion von Wahrnehmen und Erfahren von Ereignissen aus der äusseren Welt und dem Einordnen und Transformieren in die individuelle, innere Welt. Mit Assimilation bezeichnet Piaget die Eingliederung neuer Erfahrungen oder Erlebnisse in das bereits bestehende, vorhandene Wissen. Die Reize aus der Umwelt werden mit vertrauten Situationen abgeglichen und das existierende Wissen genutzt, um ähnliche Situationen einordnen zu können.[16] Stimmen die bisherigen gewonnenen Erfahrungen mit der aktuellen Situation nicht überein, ist eine Anpassung der Wahrnehmung an die Realität nötig. Diese Situation bezeichnet Piaget als Akkommodation. Das dabei gewonnene Wissen wird mit dem bereits vorhandenen abgeglichen und für weitere, ähnliche Situationen gespeichert.[17] Die individuelle Lernerfahrung ist somit durch das wechselseitige Zusammenspiel von Assimilation und Akkommodation charakterisiert.

Für Piaget verläuft die menschliche Entwicklung positiver, je mehr Möglichkeiten geboten werden, sich mit seiner Umwelt auseinanderzusetzen. Nur das Individuum selbst ist bei seiner Entwicklung aktiv. Eine optimale Lernmethode sieht deshalb für ihn die Bereitstellung von Materialien und die Schaffung von realen Problemsituationen vor, weckt Interesse und regt zu einer selbstständigen, aktiven Problemlösung an.[18]

Bauen, Beobachten und Reflektieren

Die drei theoretischen Lernmethoden von Dewey, Lewin und Piaget lassen sich mit dem Entwurfs- und Realisierungsprozess der Modellwerkstatt verknüpfen. Sie lehren, die 1:1-Aktivitäten immer im Zusammenhang von Umfeld und Individuum in einem Prozess zu sehen. Ihre Theorien lassen sich vereinfacht auf drei Arten des Lernens — „wie man etwas tut", „wie man mit und von Personen lernt" und „lernen, etwas zu lernen" — zusammenfassen. Dies schafft ein Zusammenspiel von Gefühlen, Gedanken, Erfahrungen und Empfindungen während des Bauens im Massstab 1:1.

Wie von Lewin in der Aktionsforschung postuliert, beinhaltet die Umsetzung der Modellwerkstatt alle charakteristischen und für die Aktionsforschung typischen, aufeinanderfolgenden und zusammenhängenden Prozessschritte. Dabei stellt das Bauen im Massstab 1:1 die eigentliche Aktivität dar. Das war der Moment, wo Studierende, Lehrende und Fachleute aus der Praxis gemeinsam als Gruppe die Modellwerkstatt konstruierten und bauten. Dieses Experiment im Sinne von Dewey integrierte unterschiedliche Wissensniveaus aus Theorie und Praxis und ermöglichte ein Lernen von und in der Gruppe als Team. In dieser Lernsituation wurde der Bauprozess der Modellwerkstatt von allen Beteiligten in Form von Präsentationen und Diskussionen beobachtet. Dadurch ist der Verlauf des Bauprozesses gemeinsam gesteuert und die konstruktiven Entscheidungen und gestalterischen Einflüsse sind zusammen entwickelt worden. Dies war aus Sicht der teilnehmenden Studierenden ein wichtiger Bestandteil des gemeinsamen Prozesses.

Die Beobachtung und die Reflektion erfolgten auf zwei Ebenen, während der Aktivität und nach der Aktivität. Während der 1:1-Aktivität durch Zwischen- und Schlusskritiken und das parallel zum Bauen verlaufende

Sammeln der für den Bauprozess relevanten Daten in Form von Skizzen und Plänen. Dies ermöglichte Studierenden, Lehrenden und Fachleuten, die getroffenen konstruktiven und baulichen Entscheidungen und die dabei gemachten Beobachtungen Schritt für Schritt mit Distanz in der Gruppe zu hinterfragen und bei Bedarf korrigieren zu können. Dadurch entstand über den gesamten 1:1-Prozess ein sich mehrmals wiederholender Zyklus aus Aktivität, Beobachtung und Reflexion, den Lewin als wichtiges Steuerungselement der Aktionsforschung sieht und Piaget als individuelle kognitive Erfahrung versteht.

Bauen im Massstab 1:1 ist nicht nur ein individueller, nicht nur ein intellektueller oder praktischer Vorgang, sondern beruht auf dem Zusammenspiel von vielen Faktoren. Hands-on-Aktionen ermöglichen den Teilnehmenden die Sensibilisierung ihrer eigenen Wahrnehmung, die Stärkung der Erfahrung, das Entdecken von Wissen, das Vermitteln von Handlungskompetenzen und die Intensivierung der Zusammenarbeit mit Fachleuten aus der Praxis. Die direkte Verbindung der mit Studierenden durchgeführten Hands-on-Aktivitäten beim Bau der Modellwerkstatt der Universität Liechtenstein erlaubte den teilnehmenden Studierenden auf diesem Wege, die Bereiche Praxis und Theorie spielerisch zu entdecken und mit ihrer individuellen Entwicklung zu verknüpfen. Es entstand ein lebendiger Prozess mit vielen Experimentiermöglichkeiten für die Architekturstudierenden, die sie auf ihre zukünftige Arbeitswelt vorbereiteten. Dieses Geschehen lässt sich treffend als „Lernen durch Erfahrung"[19] kennzeichnen und ist ein zentrales didaktisches Moment beim Bauen im Massstab 1:1. *Lernen ist besser, weil intensiver als lehren: je mehr gelehrt wird, desto weniger kann gelernt werden,*[20] meinte dazu bereits Josef Albers in seinem Vorkursunterricht am Bauhaus in Dessau.

One must learn by doing the thing; for though you think you know it, you have no certainty until you try.

Sophocles[1]

In 1938, the American psychologist and educationalist John Dewey published his book on educational philosophy, *Experience and Education*. In it, he attaches great importance to experiments that are used to convey and develop learning content. In Dewey's concept, education has the primary task of nurturing one's own faculties for the new while developing an awareness of the shared. In addition to training specialist skills, experiments that are in line with his understanding also integrate equally important social and relationship skills. These include methods to manage learning effectively and to convey the skills together with subject-specific knowledge.[2] Moreover, he believes that experimentation must always be integrated into the life of the individual and society, into real surroundings.[3]

In addition to experiments, Dewey's theory of learning focuses on learning stimuli that elicit and enable positive learning. According to Dewey, learning processes that are stimulating change the learning process itself, arousing curiosity and creating a desire for concrete experiences in the form of purposeful action.[4] For Dewey, stimuli for independent judgement arise by guiding the learner's natural impulses to act through the concept of 'stop and think', the exchange of thoughts in conjunction with one's eyes and hands. Thinking is always a retrospective process of contemplating something. Self-control, according to Dewey, enables the development of one's own judgement and should therefore be taught to an increasing extent.[5]

For Dewey, education is not a finished product, but ideally prepares the learner for a lifetime of learning.[6] Lessons must be flexible in order to enable self-directed learning and independent research.[7] His theories of learning are still valid today and were far ahead of their time.

His methods of experimentation, laboratory studies and field projects were especially popular and can still be found today in curricula across a wide range of educational disciplines.[8]

Action research

Kurt Lewin and John Dewey are in agreement in their position that education must include both social justice and the democratic participation of those involved.[9] Whereas Dewey understood his learning methods more as stimuli, Lewin focused his work on processes and used them to develop new scientific methods. For Lewin, the integration of practice and theory was of great importance, which is reflected in his extensive consulting and research activities in American industry.[10]

In the 1940s, Lewin developed a special form of scientific investigation with the aim of gaining knowledge about a social system and at the same time being able to influence it.[11] He describes this procedure in his 1946 article 'Action Research and Minority Problems',[12] and in it he defines the process, from an idea to a goal, as a sequence of steps. The first step involves weighing the idea against the resources available to achieve the goal. It entails collecting data and observing the here and now. The subsequent development of an overall plan shows how the goal is to be achieved. The next step is to evaluate the initial action steps and to decide whether it is necessary to make any modifications to the action. Then the action is evaluated again and based on this, the further course of action is decided.[13] In this whole process, Lewin attaches great importance to feedback so as to be able to share and review the abstract and concrete experiences made in the research group. This sequence of planning, activity, observation and reflection, which is typical of action research, is already implied in the procedure outlined by his step-by-step reflection of the scientific investigation. Lewin remarks on this: *If we cannot judge whether an action has led forward or backward, if we have no criteria for evaluating the relation between effort and achievement, there is nothing to prevent us from making the wrong conclusions.*[14]

Assimilation and accommodation

For the Swiss psychologist and genetic epistemologist Jean Piaget, as with Kurt Lewin and John Dewey, a learning process arises from the interplay between environment and individual.[15] Piaget explains this interplay with the terms assimilation and accommodation, the reciprocal interaction of perceiving and experiencing events from the external world and integrating and transforming them into one's own individual, internal world. Piaget uses the term assimilation to identify the incorporation of new instances of know-how or experiences into the pre-existing, available pool of knowledge. Stimuli from one's surroundings are compared to familiar situations and existing knowledge is used to enable one to categorise and fully understand similar situations.[16] If the experiences gathered up to this point do not match the current situation, an adjustment is necessary to bring perceptions into line with reality. Piaget calls this situation accommodation. The knowledge gained in the process is compared with what is already available and stored for further, similar situations.[17] The individual learning experience is thus characterized by a reciprocal interplay of assimilation and accommodation.

For Piaget, the more opportunities are afforded to engage with one's environment, the more positively human development proceeds. Only the individuals themselves are active in their development. For this reason, he believes that an optimal learning method provides for the provision of materials and the creation of real problem situations, arouses interest and encourages independent, active problem solving.[18]

Building, observing and reflecting

All three different theoretical learning methods devised by Dewey, Lewin and Piaget can be linked to the process of designing and building the model workshop. They teach us to always see the full-scale activities as part of a process in the context of the wider environment and the individual. Their theories can be summarised as three types of learning: 'how to do something', 'how to learn with and from people' and 'learning to learn something'. This gives rise to an interplay of feelings, thoughts, experiences and sentiments during the process of building at full scale.

As postulated by Lewin in the concept of action research, implementing the model workshop involves all the characteristic sequential and interrelated procedural steps of action research. Building at full scale is the key activity. This was the moment when the students, teachers and expert practitioners worked together as a group to design and build the model workshop. This experiment, carried out in the spirit of Dewey, integrated different levels of knowledge from theory and practice and made it possible to learn as a team, from and in the group. In this learning situation, the process of building the model workshop was observed by all participants in the form of presentations and discussions. In this way, the progress of the construction process was jointly controlled and the design influences and construction decisions were developed in tandem. From the viewpoint of the participating students, this was an important part of the collective process.

Observation and reflection took place at two levels, during and after the activity. During the activity of full-scale construction, it took place through interim and final critiques and the compiling of data relevant to the building process, which was gathered while construction was ongoing and took the form of sketches and plans. This enabled students, teachers and experts to scrutinise, step by step, within the group, and with a degree of detachment, the decisions taken on design and construction and the observations made along the way, and to be able to correct them if necessary. This resulted in a repeatedly occurring cycle of activity, observation and reflection spanning the entire full-scale process, which Lewin sees as an important governing element of action research and Piaget sees as individual cognitive experience.

Building at full scale is not only an individual process, nor just an intellectual or practical process, but is based on the interplay of many factors. Hands-on actions enable the participants to raise their awareness of their own perceptions, strengthen their experience, discover knowledge, impart coping skills and intensify collaboration with expert practitioners. The direct experience of the hands-on activities carried out by the students while building the model workshop at the University of Liechtenstein allowed the participating students to discover both practice and theory in a playful way and to relate these to their personal development. What emerged was a spirited process with many opportunities for the architecture students to experiment, preparing them for their future work environment. This process can be aptly described as 'learning through experience'[19] and is a central didactic moment in building at full scale. *Learning is better than teaching because it is more intensive: the more we teach, the less students can learn.*[20] That was Josef Albers's opinion on the matter in his preliminary course at the Bauhaus in Dessau.

Modellwerkstatt Studio Model Workshop Studio 34

Materialbewusstsein und Tektonik
Material Consciousness and Tectonics

Carmen Rist-Stadelmann

Tektonik ist also die Lehre vom Zusammenfügen von Einzelteilen zu einem Ganzen, zu einem Gebilde der Baukunst, wenn man will: die Lehre vom inneren Aufbau eines Kunstwerkes. Tektonik als ästhetischer Ausdruck konstruktiver Gesetzmässigkeiten verlangt nach einer Baukonstruktion, die sich nicht einfach von der Tätigkeit des entwerfenden Architekten abspalten oder sich von der künstlerischen Bewältigung des Bauens getrennt betrachten lässt.

Hans Kollhoff [1]

Der architektonische Entwurfs- und Realisierungsprozess ist charakterisiert durch seine Komplexität, die durch permanente Koordinationsabläufe mit den am Bau beteiligten Akteuren entsteht. Viele Einzelteile sind in diesem baulichen Zusammenspiel zu berücksichtigen, bevor ein neues Ganzes entsteht. Materialien wirken dabei wie kleine Zahnrädchen in einer grossen Maschine. Um Architekturstudierende mit diesem Prozess vertraut zu machen und sie auf ihr zukünftiges Berufsleben vorzubereiten, bietet sich das Bauen im Massstab 1:1 an. Das sogenannte Hands-on ermöglicht weitreichende Erfahrungsmöglichkeiten, angefangen von gestalterischen über technische, bauphysikalische und konstruktive Aspekte bis hin zu Teamarbeit. Dabei gilt es, die Freude und Neugierde am Zusammenspiel von Gestalt und Konstruktion zu wecken und als Symbiose von Kunst und Technik zu verstehen. Oder anders gesagt, das Material als Treiber, als architektonischen Ursprung von Gestalt und Konstruktion zu kultivieren. Indem wir Material in den Fokus der 1:1-Aktivitäten von gebauten Objekten oder Materialexperimenten stellen, schaffen wir die Möglichkeit, dies zu erfahren.

Kultur des Fügens

Die Kunst des logischen Fügens der Materialien vom Einzelteil zu einem neuen Ganzen geriet im Laufe der Geschichte seit der Industrialisierung und bis heute mit der Digitalisierung in Vergessenheit. Durch diesen Verlust ist das Zusammenspiel von Gestalt und Konstruktion nach den Eigenschaften der Materialien vielfach nicht mehr gegeben. Um die Kultur des Fügens und das Wechselspiel von Kunst und Technik in der Architekturausbildung wieder zu beleben und zu thematisieren, bietet sich die Tektonik mit ihrer implizierten Hierarchie in der Konstruktion und in der Fügung vom Groben zum Feinen direkt an.

Dieses Zusammenfügen von starren, stabförmigen Teilen zu einem in sich unverrückbaren System ist für Gottfried Semper unstreitig das Wichtigste und zugleich auch Schwierigste, wie er in „Der Stil in den technischen und tektonischen Künsten"[2] erklärt. Für die tektonische Fügung ist von Bedeutung, dass Architektur immer Tragwerk plus Verkleidung ist, wobei der Einsatz der Materialien konstruktiv bedingt ist und somit Gestalt und Konstruktion zu einer Einheit zusammengeführt sind. Die Erscheinung entspricht somit auch der Technik. Adolf Loos schreibt dazu: *Das Princip der Bekleidung, das zuerst von Semper ausgesprochen wurde, erstreckt sich auch auf die Natur. Der Mensch ist mit einer Haut, der Baum mit einer Rinde bekleidet.*[3] Diese Analogie der Tektonik zur menschlichen Anatomie zeigt auf, dass die Haut als Bekleidung immer konstruktiv mit dem Inneren des Menschen verbunden ist, sie ist Teil unseres Körpers. Bedeutend für Loos ist deshalb, dass die Bekleidung nicht mit bekleidenden Materialien verwechselt werden darf. *Dieses Gesetz also lautet: Die Möglichkeit, das bekleidete Material mit der Bekleidung verwechseln zu können, soll auf alle Fälle ausgeschlossen sein.*[4] Um die unterschiedlichsten Materialien im tektonischen Verständnis zu fügen, braucht es Grundkenntnisse von den zur Anwendung kommenden Materialien.

Kultivierung des Materials

Um diese Grundkenntnisse zu erlangen, braucht es Materialbewusstsein und vor allem Wissen und Erfahrungen über ihre Eigenschaften und

Einsatzmöglichkeiten. Denn wie Loos treffend beschreibt, sind nicht alle Materialien gleich. *Ein jedes Material hat seine eigene Formsprache und kein Material kann die Form eines anderen Materials für sich in Anspruch nehmen. Denn die Formen haben sich aus der Verwendbarkeit und Herstellungsweise eines jeden Materials gebildet, die sind mit dem Material und durch das Material geworden.*[5]

Materialbewusstsein gliedert Richard Sennett in seinem Buch „Handwerk" in drei Phasen.[6] Die erste Phase bezeichnet er als „Metamorphose", die Veränderung des Materials. Diese entsteht für ihn durch die Weiterentwicklung des Materials zu einer Typenform, der Bildung eines Urteils über dessen Mischung in Kombination von Formen und im Nachdenken über den Anwendungsbereich.[7] Die zweite Phase des Materialbewusstseins bezeichnet er als „Präsenz". Sie entsteht für ihn durch die Bearbeitung, in der Herstellungszeichen hinterlassen werden, das Material markiert wird oder Fertigungsprozesse sichtbar sind, also durch die Bearbeitung des Materials wie z. B. ein Stempel bei Ziegeln, und wie es anschliessend zueinander gefügt wird.[8] Als „Anthropomorphose" bzw. als dritten Bereich des Materialbewusstseins bezeichnet es Sennett, wenn einem unbearbeiteten Stoff menschliche Qualitäten zugeschrieben werden. Wenn von echtem Material oder schönem Material gesprochen wird, also wenn dem Gebauten menschliche Züge und Eigenschaften zugeordnet werden.[9] Materialbewusstsein nach Sennett bedeutet in der Architekturausbildung, dass Studierende bereits während des Studiums mit unterschiedlichen Materialien und ihren unterschiedlichen Aggregatzuständen vertraut gemacht werden sollten. Sie müssen wissen, wie die jeweiligen Materialien bearbeitet werden können, wie sie weiterentwickelt und vom Kleinen ins Grosse tektonisch gefügt werden. Kurzum, wie sie, ihren Eigenschaften entsprechend, zur baulichen Anwendung kommen, und wie dieses Zusammenspiel am Ende die gebaute Erscheinung langfristig prägt.

Materialbewusstsein lässt sich aber nicht nur auf Materialeigenschaften, Herstellungs- und Werkzeugspuren begrenzen, sondern integriert auch tektonisches und strukturelles Wissen. Zum Materialbewusstsein gehört deshalb eine empirische Kombination aus manueller Erfahrung und geistiger Reflexion, welche kaum voneinander zu trennen sind.

Zusammenspiel von Hand und Kopf

Die Verbindung der geistigen Reflektion und der manuellen Tätigkeit kommt beim Bauen im Massstab 1:1 ganz natürlich zum Tragen. Zu diesem Zusammenspiel von Kopf und Hand gelangen wir, indem wir neben dem theoretischen Wissen auch mit den eigenen Händen arbeiten und entwerfen. Dies bedeutet, dass alles theoretisch erlernte Wissen im Kopf gespeichert ist und mit den Händen in die Praxis umgesetzt werden kann. Beim Bauen im Massstab 1:1 wird dieses Wechselspiel von Wissen aus Theorie und Praxis, sozusagen Auge und Hand, miteinander vertraut gemacht. Dabei erfolgt die Sensibilisierung über das haptische Erfahren des Körpers. Die Hand berührt das Material mit dem Daumen, wiegt es auf der Handfläche und erfasst es mit der ganzen Hand. Die Finger spüren, die Hände greifen und tasten und das Zusammenspiel von Hand-Handgelenk-Unterarm handelt im Ganzen. Der Informationsaustausch zwischen Auge und Hand wird durch Wiederholungen gestärkt. Die Hand muss zuerst an den Fingerspitzen sensibilisiert werden, danach kann sie sich dem Problem der Koordination zuwenden, danach erfolgt die Integration der Hand in Gelenk und Unterarm. Juhani Pallasmaa beschreibt diesen Prozess treffend: *For the sportsman, craftsman, magician and artist alike, the seamless and unconscious collaboration of the eye, hand and mind is crucial. As the performance is gradually perfected, perception, action of the hand and the thought lose their independence and turn into a singular and subliminally coordinated system of reaction and response.*[10]

Diese Art des Sehens, das Zusammenspiel von Hand und Kopf, lehrten Josef Albers und László Moholy-Nagy durch sogenannte „Tastübungen" im Vorkurs am Weimarer Bauhaus. In diesen Übungen stellten Studierende unterschiedliche Materialeigenschaften visuell und haptisch zusammen. Die Materialklaviatur ging dabei von hart-weich zu glatt-rau, klar-trüb, engmaschig-weitmaschig usw. Diese Übung hatte keine wissenschaftliche oder konstruktionstechnische Absicht, sondern zum Ziel, Erfahrungen über die Materialien zu sammeln, um diese auf dem Gebiet des Bauens anschliessend adaptieren und umsetzten zu können.[11] Material muss laut Albers respektiert werden: *Find a relationship between the material and the form it will take, so that the result expresses something of the material's character.*[12] Diese Haltung bezieht sich nicht nur auf das Material selber, sondern beinhaltet für Albers auch die Wahl des Werkzeuges. Die ausführende Hand spielt dabei eine wichtige Rolle, da sie das Material mit dem jeweiligen Werkzeug oder der Maschine bearbeitet. Das Werkzeug ist die Verlängerung der Hand, das beim Bauen im Massstab 1:1 Produktionsspuren erzeugt. Diese Spuren der Interaktion von Werkzeug und Produktion sind bei Holz, dem verwendeten Material beim Bau der Modellwerkstatt, besonders gut sichtbar. Angefangen von sägerau über poliert bis geschliffen, spiegeln sie immer das verwendete Werkzeug wider und geben dadurch Auskunft über den Herstellungsprozess.

Material und Experiment

Während des Entwerfens und Bauens an der Modellwerkstatt waren Materialbewusstsein, Tektonik und Materialexperimente von grosser Bedeutung. Als Teil des Prozesses standen sie im Zentrum der Aktivität. Material als Gesamtes, als Einheit von Gestalt und Konstruktion wahrzunehmen und als Treiber, als Ursprung von Gestalt und Konstruktion den Studierenden verständlich zu machen, wurde bewusst kultiviert. Dadurch entstand ein Materialbewusstsein in den Stufen von Sennett. Parallel dazu kam dem tektonischen Fügen, vom Einzelnen zu einem neuen Ganzen im Sinne Sempers, eine wichtige Bedeutung zu. Materialübungen sensibilisierten im Sinne Albers für die Symbiose von Kopf und Hand und begeisterten die Studierenden für das Zusammenspiel von Kunst und Technik.

Der Einsatz und die Verwendung der Materialien prägen die Gestalt und Erscheinung unserer gebauten Architektur. Deshalb ist es von grosser Bedeutung, den bewussten Materialumgang bereits in der Architekturausbildung als Schwerpunkt zu vertiefen. Den tektonischen Diskurs zu leben, die materielle Sensibilisierung zu fördern, das Zusammenspiel von Kopf und Hand zu kultivieren, kurzum, die Freude und Neugierde am Zusammenspiel von Material, seiner Gestalt und Konstruktion, also der Symbiose von Kunst und Technik im Entwurfs- und Realisierungsprozess zu wecken.

Tectonics is therefore the study of joining individual parts together to make up a whole, to create an object of architecture, if you will: it is the study of the inner structure of an artwork. Tectonics, as the aesthetic expression of laws of construction, demands a structural design that cannot be easily separated from the work of the architect who designs it, nor can it be considered separately from the artistic mastery of building.

Hans Kollhoff[1]

The process of architectural design and construction is characterised by a complexity that stems from unending processes of coordination that take place among all those involved in building. Many individual aspects have to be taken into account in this collaborative process of construction in order for a new whole to emerge. Building materials function like tiny cogs in a big machine. Building at full scale is an ideal way to familiarise architecture students with this process and to prepare them for their future professional career. The so-called hands-on approach allows for a wide range of experiences, ranging from the design-related to the more technical, including matters of building physics and construction, to teamwork. The aim is to awaken a sense of joy and curiosity about the interplay between form and construction, and to understand it as the symbiosis between art and technology. Or, to put in other terms, to cultivate the notion of material as a driving force, as the architectural origin of design and construction. By making materials the central focus of our experiments and activities building full-size objects, we create the opportunity to experience this.

The culture of assembly

The art of assembling materials logically, of joining individual parts to create a new whole, has become forgotten over the course of history, starting with industrialisation and continuing to the digitalisation of the present. Due to this loss, the interplay between design and construction in response to the properties of materials is, in many cases, no longer a given. As a means to revive and address the culture of assembly and the interplay of art and technology in architectural education, tectonics, with its implied hierarchy of construction and assembly, lends itself to direct application at every scale from the coarse to the fine.

This joining of rigid, rod-like parts to create a system that is inherently immutable is, for Gottfried Semper, indisputably the most important and at the same time most difficult task, as he explains in *Style in the Technical and Tectonic Arts*.[2] Important to tectonic assembly is that architecture is always a load-bearing structure plus cladding, where the use of materials is determined by construction, and thus design and construction are combined to form a single whole. Thus the outward appearance also corresponds to the technology used. Adolf Loos writes: *The principle of cladding, which was first articulated by Semper, extends to nature as well. Man is covered with skin, the tree with bark.*[3] This analogy between tectonics and human anatomy shows that the skin as cladding is always joined constructively with a person's insides; it is part of our body. That is why Loos finds it important that the cladding must not be confused with the materials used for the cladding. *The law goes like this: we must work in such a way that a confusion of the material clad with its cladding is impossible.*[4] In order to join highly diverse materials in a tectonic way, one needs a basic knowledge of the materials to be used.

Cultivating the material

To acquire this basic knowledge, one needs an awareness of materials and, above all, knowledge and experience about their properties and potential uses. Because, as Loos aptly said, not all materials are alike. *Every material possesses its own language of forms, and none may lay claim for itself to the forms of another material. For forms have been constituted out of the applicability and the methods of production of materials. They have come into being with and through materials.*[5]

In his book *The Craftsman*, Richard Sennett divides material consciousness into three phases.[6] He describes the first phase as 'metamorphosis', a transformation of the material. For him, this metamorphosis takes place by developing the material further into a 'type-form', establishing a judgement about its intermixture within a combination of forms and in consideration of the domain in which it is used.[7] He identifies the second phase of material consciousness as 'presence'. For him, this emerges from the processing, during which production marks are left behind, the material is marked or manufacturing processes become made visible; in other words, through the processing of the material (such as pressing a stamp into bricks) and how it is subsequently assembled.[8] The 'anthropomorphosis', the third area of material consciousness, is described by Sennett as what happens when an unprocessed material is ascribed human qualities. This is when we speak of real material or beautiful material, that is, when built things are assigned human traits and properties.[9] With respect to architectural education, material consciousness as defined by Sennett means that even during their studies, students should be introduced to a variety of materials and their different aggregate states. They need to know how different materials can be processed, how they can be developed further and tectonically assembled from small to large. In brief, students should learn how to use various materials to build in accordance with their properties and how this interplay ultimately has a lasting impact on the built appearance.

Material consciousness cannot be limited to material properties and the traces of production and tools, however; it also integrates tectonic and structural knowledge. Material consciousness involves an empirical combination of manual experience and intellectual reflection that can hardly be separated from each other.

Interaction of hand and mind

The combination of intellectual reflection and manual activity comes to fruition naturally when building at full scale. We arrive at this interplay of mind and hand by working and designing not only with theoretical knowledge but also with our own hands. This means that all theoretically learned knowledge is stored in our minds and can be put into practice with our hands. When building at full scale, knowledge from both theory and practice—acquired, as it were, by the eye and the hand—are combined and brought into harmony with each other. And awareness is raised through the haptic experience of the body. The hand touches the material with the thumb, cradles it in the palm of the hand and grasps it with the entire hand. The fingers touch, the hands grasp and feel, and the collaboration between hand, wrist and lower arm acts as a whole. The exchange of information between eye and hand is strengthened by repetitions. The hand must first be made aware by the tips of the fingers. After that, it can turn to the problem of coordination, and then comes the integration of the hand into wrist and lower arm. Juhani Pallasmaa aptly describes this process: *For the sportsman, craftsman, magician and artist alike, the seamless and unconscious collaboration of the eye, hand and mind is crucial. As the performance is gradually perfected, perception, action of the hand and the thought lose their independence and turn into a singular and subliminally coordinated system of reaction and response.*[10]

This way of seeing, the synergy of hand and mind, was taught by Josef Albers and László Moholy-Nagy through so-called 'tactile exercises' in the preliminary course at the Weimar Bauhaus. In these exercises, students assembled different material properties together based on their visual and haptic qualities. The gamut of materials went from hard to soft, smooth to rough, clear to cloudy, close-meshed to wide-meshed, and so on. This exercise had no ambitions related to science or construction; rather, the aim was to gain experience about the materials in order to then adapt and implement them in the realm of construction.[11] According to Albers, material must be respected: *Find a relationship between the material and the form it will take, so that the result expresses something of the material's character.*[12] For Albers, this stance not only pertains to the material itself but also includes the choice of the tool. Here, the hand carrying out the work plays an important role, as it processes the material with the respective tool or machine. The tool is an extension of the hand, which creates traces of production when building at full scale. These traces of the interaction between tools and production are particularly visible in the case of wood, the material used to build the model workshop. From rough-sawn to polished or honed, the materials always reflect the tool used and thus provide information about the manufacturing process.

Material and experiment

While going about designing and building the model workshop, material awareness, tectonics and experiments with materials were of great importance. As part of the process, the materials were at the heart of the activity. To perceive of material as a whole, as a unity of design and construction, and to make it understandable to students as a driving force, as the origin of design and construction, was consciously cultivated. This brought about material consciousness in the phases outlined by Sennett. Parallel to this, great importance was given to tectonic assembly—joining individual parts to a new whole, in the spirit of Semper. Material exercises raised the students' awareness of the symbiosis of mind and hand as understood by Albers and inspired them for the interplay of art and technology.

The deployment and use of materials influence the design and outward appearance of our built architecture. So it is of great importance to begin gathering in-depth experience with how to consciously deal with materials early on during one's architectural studies. It is about living the tectonic discourse, fostering a sensitivity for materials, cultivating the interplay between mind and hand; in short, about generating a sense of joy and curiosity about the interplay of materials, their design and construction, that is, the symbiosis between art and technology in the process of designing and building.

Modellwerkstatt Studio Model Workshop Studio

Handwerk als kollektiver Prozess
Craft as a Collective Process

Carmen Rist-Stadelmann

Learning is best conceived as a process, not in terms of outcomes.

David Kolb[1]

Unsere heutige Vorstellung von Handwerk ist laut David Pye immer noch stark geprägt von den Idealen der „Arts and Crafts"-Bewegung, die ihren Ursprung im Protest gegen die Prozesse und Ästhetik der industriellen Produktion rund um William Morris hatte.[2] Der grosse Kritiker der industriellen Revolution fand die ideale Zusammenarbeit zwischen Kunst und Handwerk im Mittelalter. In den mittelalterlichen Werkstätten erfolgte die gemeinsame Ausbildung von Handwerkern und „Künstlern". Beide durchliefen dieselbe Ausbildung in verschiedenen Stufen, vom Lehrling über den Gesellen bis zum Meister. In Morris' Verständnis war im Mittelalter jeder Künstler ein Handwerker und jeder Handwerker ein Künstler. Dass im Mittelalter hochwertige Dinge für den Alltag hergestellt werden konnten, liegt seiner Meinung nach an der Freude an der Arbeit und am Handwerk selber. Wenn die Freude an der Arbeit verloren geht, hat das Kunsthandwerk keinen Wert mehr. Durch seine Leidenschaft für das Selbermachen belebte er die Bereiche des Handwerks neu. Dieser Einfluss auf das Handwerk ist als „Arts and Crafts"-Bewegung bekannt geworden.[3]

Morris' handwerkliche Vorstellungen und die damit verbundenen „Arts and Crafts"-Ideen breiteten sich von England rasch auf dem Kontinent aus und fanden grossen Widerhall. Dies führte zur Bildung von diversen Werkstätten wie z. B. der Wiener, Münchner oder Dresdner Werkstätten. Das Ziel dieser Werkstätten war es, handwerklich hochwertige und der Zeit entsprechend moderne Produkte zu entwerfen und zu produzieren.[4]

Werkstatt als Ausbildungsort

William Morris' gelebte handwerkliche Symbiose von Kunst und Handwerk veränderte auch das Bild und Verständnis der Architekturausbildung, die bis ins 18. Jahrhundert an Akademien als etablierte Ausbildungsorte erfolgte. Im Laufe des 19. Jahrhunderts verloren die Akademien zunehmend an Bedeutung, da sie auf das neue technische Verständnis und den Einfluss der Industrialisierung nicht zu reagieren wussten. Sie erhielten den Ruf, zu wenig praxisorientiert, verstaubt und keine zeitgemässe Ausbildungsstätte mehr zu sein. Sie galten als Elfenbeinturm mit Reproduktionscharakter, mit deren Hilfe sich der Historismus etablieren konnte.[5] Aus dieser zunehmenden Ablehnung gegenüber den Akademien erklärte sich der verstärkte Wunsch nach einer praxisbezogenen Ausbildung mit der Verbindung eines theoretischen und akademischen Unterrichts mit praktischer Unterrichtsgestaltung. Bereits Gottfried Semper beklagte die Trennung von Kunst und Handwerk.[6] Er drängte auf eine erneute Verknüpfung von Theorie und Praxis in der Architekturausbildung und hob besonders die Wichtigkeit von Technik und Materialkenntnissen hervor. Sein Wunsch nach einer einheitlichen Ausbildung von Kunst und Handwerk war, ähnlich wie bei Morris, geprägt von den mittelalterlichen Werkstattgemeinschaften.[7]

So ist es nicht überraschend, dass Morris' handwerkliche Ideen auf fruchtbaren Boden fielen, um die Trennung zwischen Kunst und Handwerk, Praxis und Theorie in der Ausbildung wieder aufzuheben.[8] Unter diesem Einfluss entstanden in England zahlreiche neue Schulen, die eine geistige Ausbildung auf handwerklichen Grundlagen unter dem Schlagwort „Technical Education" integrierten und in ihrem Curriculum anboten. Handwerker und sogenannte Dilettanten wurden wie im Vorbild der mittelalterlichen Werkstätten zeitgleich unterrichtet. Im Zuge dieser Erneuerung hielten Werkstätten Einzug in die Ausbildungsorte, wie z. B. die Central School of Arts and Crafts in der Londoner Regent-Street zeigt.[9]

Diese Art des Unterrichtens hatte auch grossen Einfluss im deutschsprachigen Raum. Anfang des 20. Jahrhunderts führten dies Henry Van de Velde in Weimar, Hans Poelzig in Breslau und Hermann Muthesius in den Preussischen Kunstgewerbeschulen ein.[10] Aber nicht nur im deutschsprachigen Raum hielten Werkstätten in den Ausbildungsort Einzug. Mit dem russischen Labor der Moderne, den WChUTEMAS in Russland, wurde von 1920 bis 1930 dieser Ausbildungstyp etabliert.[11] Diese Veränderungen in der Ausbildung waren getragen von der Einsicht, die Möglichkeiten des Materials und die Gesetze der Form, wie es Semper vorausschauend gefordert hatte, in den Werkstätten handwerklich zu erfahren.[12] Allen diesen Anfang des 20. Jahrhunderts entstandenen Ausbildungsorten ist gemeinsam, dass sie mit ihrem Wunsch nach einer gelebten Verbindung von Handwerk und Kunst dem Elfenbeinturm der Akademien entkommen wollten.

Manuelle Praxis

Im Verständnis der 1:1-Aktivitäten ist Handwerk ein manueller Prozess, der Erfahrungen mit dem Material ermöglicht und die damit verbundenen Abläufe verständlich macht. Als Teil der Bauprozesse sind manuelle Aktivitäten nahe an der Realität und schliessen die Lücke zwischen Ausbildung und Berufswelt. Diese Art von Prozess erlaubt den Studierenden, Hands-on-Erfahrungen mit dem Material zu gewinnen und die damit verbundenen handwerklichen Abläufe besser kennenzulernen. Zudem ermöglicht es ihnen, handwerkliche Erfahrungen ohne grossen maschinellen und digitalen Aufwand zu sammeln.

Aus diesem Grund waren die 1:1-Aktivitäten zum Bau der Modellwerkstatt der Universität Liechtenstein so konzipiert, dass die Studierenden mit ihren eigenen Händen bauen und den Realisierungsprozess begreifen konnten. Dies wurde unter Anleitung und in gelebter Zusammenarbeit mit lokalen Handwerkern erreicht. Dabei standen nicht Präzision und fachliche Qualifikation des Handwerks, wie es ein gelernter Handwerker kann, im Vordergrund. Vielmehr lag der Fokus der Aktivitäten darin, auf eine manuelle Weise ohne industriellen Aufwand handwerkliche Aspekte miteinzubeziehen. Dies war nur durch die enge Kooperation mit den involvierten Handwerkern möglich, da diese mit ihrem manuellen und industriellen Wissen aus der Praxis die eigenen Erfahrungen der Studierenden ergänzten. Dabei blieben die involvierten Studierenden immer Teil des Herstellungsprozesses. Zusätzlich wurde der Prozess des Herstellens durch den starken Fokus auf das Material, seine Eigenschaften und die Tektonik als Themenschwerpunkt vertieft und charakterisiert. Die Studierenden waren Teil der manuellen und handwerklichen Praxis und lernten dadurch. Diese direkte Kooperation mit den Handwerksbetrieben und ihren Mitarbeitern war das Besondere am Entwurfs- und Realisierungsprozess der Modellwerkstatt und hebt diese Aktivitäten von anderen universitäreren 1:1-Projekten ab.

1:1-Werkstatt

Am Institut für Architektur und Raumentwicklung sind wir in der glücklichen Lage, dass in der Region der Universität Liechtenstein Handwerksbetriebe vorhanden sind, die unsere langjährigen 1:1-Aktivitäten auf vielfältige Weise unterstützen. Je nach Aufgabe oder Projekt können die Studierenden auf dem Firmengelände produzieren und arbeiten, oder die Unternehmen schicken ihre Handwerker zu unseren Standorten. Diesen eigens für die Hands-on-Aktivitäten der Studierenden eingerichteten temporären 1:1-Werkstätten ist gemeinsam, dass sie die theoretische und akademische Ausbildung erweitern und, den Idealen von Morris entsprechend, wie eine mittelalterliche Werkstatt funktionieren. In ihr entwerfen, produzieren und fertigen Studierende und Handwerker gemeinsam. Durch diesen einzigartigen Werkstattcharakter ist das Wissen für die Studierenden praxisorientiert und vom konstruktiven und technischen Standpunkt her aktuell.

Durch den 1:1-Entwurfs- und Realisierungsprozess der Modellwerkstatt entstand ein realer Praxisbezug und kein künstliches Uni-Labor, wo die

Studierenden in einem geschlossenen Umfeld unter sich arbeiten. Studierende und Handwerker lernten gegenseitig voneinander. Das Entwerfen, Herstellen und Produzieren passierte nicht in der Isoliertheit der akademischen Welt. Dies ermöglichte den Studierenden, die Zusammenhänge von Kunst und Handwerk zu sehen und verstehen zu lernen und in weiterer Folge ihre dabei gewonnenen Erfahrungen in die Architektur zu transformieren. Zudem lernten die Studierenden, mit Handwerkern zu kommunizieren und zu arbeiten, was eine gute Vorbereitung für das zukünftige Arbeitsleben darstellt, wie mehrere Studierende anmerkten. Die interviewten Firmeneigentümer betonten dabei auch den Mehrwert, den diese Zusammenarbeit für sie hatte, sei es durch die Ideenvielfalt der Studierenden oder die Möglichkeit, das eigene Handwerk den Studierenden näherzubringen. Zugleich ermöglichte der Bau der Modellwerkstatt, das Handwerk als manuellen Prozess wieder verstärkt in die Architekturausbildung zu integrieren und dabei langfristig die verloren gegangene Wertschätzung für das Handwerk zurückzugewinnen.

Learning is best conceived as a process, not in terms of outcomes.

David Kolb[1]

According to David Pye, our current notion of craft is still strongly influenced by the Arts and Crafts movement, which originated around William Morris in protests against the processes and aesthetics of industrial production.[2] This great critic of the Industrial Revolution saw the Middle Ages as exhibiting the ideal correspondence between arts and crafts. In medieval workshops, craftsmen and 'artists' were trained side by side. Both underwent the same training though a sequence of stages, from apprentice to journeyman to master. As Morris saw it, in the Middle Ages every artist was a craftsperson and every craftsperson was an artist. In his opinion, the fact that high-quality items for everyday life could be produced in the Middle Ages testifies to the joy found in labour and in craft itself. Once the joy of work is lost, handcrafting no longer has any value. It was through Morris's own passion for making things that he revitalised the manual crafts. This influence on handcraft became known as the Arts and Crafts movement.[3]

Morris's beliefs regarding handcraft and the associated Arts and Crafts ideas spread rapidly from England across continental Europe, where they found great resonance. This led to the formation of various workshops and artisans' collectives, such as those in Vienna, Munich and Dresden. The aim of these workshops was to design and produce handcrafted products of high quality that were suitably modern for the times.[4]

The workshop as locus of training

William Morris's lived symbiosis of art and craft also changed the image and perceptions of architectural education, which up until the 18th century took place at academies that served as established venues for training.

Over the course of the 19th century, these academies increasingly lost their importance because they didn't know how to react to new ideas of technology and the influence of industrialisation. They acquired a reputation for being insufficiently practice-oriented, for being outmoded and for no longer being contemporary enough. They were regarded as ivory towers with a cookie-cutter mentality, through which historicism gained a strong foothold.[5] This growing rejection of the academies led to increased calls for more practice-based education that combined theoretical and academic instruction with hands-on learning. Gottfried Semper had already lamented the separation of art and craft.[6] He called for renewing the link between theory and practice in architectural education and particularly emphasised the importance of technology and knowledge of materials. His desire for unified training in arts and crafts was, much like with Morris, strongly influenced by the medieval workshop guilds.[7]

So it is not surprising that Morris's ideas about craft fell on such fertile ground in the attempt to overcome the segregation between art and craft, and between practice and theory, in education.[8] Under this influence, numerous new schools emerged in England that integrated an intellectual education on the basis of skilled manual work, offered in their curriculum under the rubric of 'technical education'. Craftspeople and so-called dilettantes were taught their skills side by side just as in the model of the medieval workshops. In the course of this revival, physical workshops found their way into educational establishments, as seen, for example, at the Central School of Arts and Crafts on London's Regent Street.[9]

This type of instruction was also very influential in German-speaking countries. It was introduced at the beginning of the 20th century by Henry Van de Velde in Weimar, Hans Poelzig in Breslau and Hermann Muthesius in the Prussian schools of arts and crafts.[10] It was not only in German-speaking countries, however, that workshops found their way into places of education. This type of training became established from 1920 to 1930 at the Vkhutemas, Russia's laboratory of modernity.[11] These changes in education were borne by the insight, as foreseen by Semper's prescient demands, that the potential uses of materials and the laws of form were best experienced through hands-on activity in workshops.[12] What all these training centres that emerged in the early 20th century had in common was the endeavour to distance themselves from the ivory tower of the academies by striving to find a lived connection between craft and art.

Manual praxis

Constructing at full scale is an activity that sees handcrafting as a manual process that provides experience with a material and comprehension of the processes associated with it. Implemented as part of a construction process, these first-hand activities are close to reality and thus narrow the gap between education and the professional world. This type of exercise enables students to gain hands-on experience with materials and to become better acquainted with the artisanal processes involved. Moreover, it enables them to gain hands-on experience without the need to learn a great deal about machines and digital technology.

For this reason, the full-scale activities for realising the model workshop at the University of Liechtenstein were conceived to allow the students to build with their own hands and fully grasp the implementation process. This was achieved under the guidance of and in lived close cooperation with local craftspeople. The focus thereby was not on achieving the precision and technical qualification of manual work on a par with what a skilled craftsperson can do. Rather, the focus of the activities was on incorporating aspects of craft in a hands-on way and without industrial input. This was only possible through close cooperation with the participating craftspeople, whose practical knowledge, both manual and industrial, added to the students' first-hand experiences. In the course of this activity, the students who took part remained active in the entire production process. In addition, the process of making was reinforced and characterised by a thematic focus aimed strongly at the material, its properties and the tectonics. The students were part of, and learned from, the practical experience of doing manual and skilled work. This direct cooperation with the building trade firms and their employees is what was special about the process of designing and building the model workshop and it differentiates these activities from other full-scale university projects.

Full-scale workshop

We at the Institute of Architecture and Planning are fortunate to have building trade firms in the region around the University of Liechtenstein that support our long-standing full-scale activities in a variety of ways. Depending on the task or project, students can produce and work on the companies' premises, or the businesses send their craftspeople to our sites. What these temporary full-scale workshops—set up specifically for the students' hands-on activities—have in common is that they augment the theoretical and academic training and, in keeping with Morris's ideals, function like a medieval workshop. They enable students and craftspeople to design, produce and make things together. Thanks to this unique workshop character, the knowledge gained by the students is practical and up-to-date from both a constructional and a technical point of view.

The process of designing and building the model workshop at full scale —as opposed to working an artificial university laboratory, where students are amongst themselves in a closed environment—provided a real-life application of practical relevance. The students and craftspeople learned from one another. The acts of designing, making and producing did not happen in the isolation of the academic world. This enabled the students to learn to see and understand the interrelationships between art and craft, and then to transform their experiences into architecture. In addition, the students learned to communicate and work with craftspeople, which, as several students noted, is good preparation for their future professional lives. When interviewed, the owners of the participating building trade firms also emphasised the added value they gained from the collaboration, be it through the diversity of the students' ideas or the chance to give students a better understanding of their craft. At the same time, building the model workshop made it possible to reintegrate craft as a manual process into the architectural education to a greater extent and, in the long term, to regain the lost appreciation for craft.

Zwischenkritik, Modellwerkstatt Studio
Mid-Term Reviews, Model Workshop Studio

Zwischenkritik, Modellwerkstatt Studio
Mid-Term Reviews, Model Workshop Studio

Bei der Modellwerkstatt gab es keinen fertigen Entwurf, nach dem gebaut werden konnte. Wir haben experimentiert, gezeichnet, ausprobiert und gebaut zur gleichen Zeit. Es war ein umgekehrtes Bauen.

Viviane Göbel
MSc Studierende

With the model workshop, there was no finished design to build from. We experimented, drew, tested and built at one and the same time. It was building in reverse.

Viviane Göbel
MSc student

Methoden des Bauens
Methods of Building

Carmen Rist-Stadelmann
Urs Meister

Every time man uses his know-how / His experience increases / And his intellectual advantages / Automatically increases. / Because of its conservation / Energy cannot decrease. / Know-how can only increase.

Buckminster Fuller[1]

Die heutige Differenzierung, Spezialisierung und Mechanisierung der beruflichen Tätigkeiten sind mit dem Beginn des Industriezeitalters und seiner Weiterentwicklung entstanden. Von der Trennung von Handwerk und Kunst über die Aufteilung der Baukunst in eine Welt der gestaltenden Architektur und berechnenden Ingenieurwissenschaft bis zur Arbeitsübernahme durch unsere aktuellen digitalen Erneuerungen. Laut Laszlo Moholy-Nagy entsteht dadurch ein Zustand in der Ausbildungskultur, der einen „sektorhaften Menschen" schafft, der an seiner gesamtheitlichen Entwicklung gehindert wird.[2] Für Juhani Pallasmaa fragmentiert diese Zunahme an Spezialisierung die Architektur, die Architekturidentität sowie den Arbeitsprozess und schwächt schliesslich das gebaute Resultat. Er kritisiert die damit einhergehende zunehmende Distanz zwischen dem Praktischen und dem Intellektuellen, dem Studio und der Baustelle. Für Pallasmaa zeichnet der Architekt heute aus der sicheren Distanz im Studio an seinen Plänen. Er agiert mehr wie ein Anwalt, der seine Fälle aus der Kanzlei bearbeitet, und entdeckt dabei nicht mehr das Material und involviert nicht die physischen Prozesse des Machens in seine Überlegungen.[3] Diese Trennung wird durch den Vormarsch des Computers und die damit einhergehende Digitalisierung unterstützt, welche diese traditionellen Prozesse kontinuierlich verändert. Es ist daher kein Wunder, dass aktuell der Wunsch nach Einbindung der Praxis in verschiedenen Facetten in die Architekturausbildung laut wird, um den Hands-on-Prozessen wieder vermehrt Raum zu gegeben.

Impulse des Machens

Das Bestreben, manuelle Tätigkeiten als praxisorientierten Teil in die Ausbildung zu integrieren, um auf das zukünftige Berufsleben gut vorbereitet zu sein, ist nicht nur eine Tendenz unserer heutigen Zeit und darf, wie ein Blick in die Geschichte der Pädagogik zeigt, nicht isoliert betrachtet werden.

Einer der Ersten, der den erzieherischen Wert von handwerklichem Tun erkannte, war der Engländer John Locke.[4] In seiner Vorstellung bringt manuelles Tun einen gesunden Geist in einem gesunden Körper hervor. Die handwerklichen Fertigkeiten müssen nicht für das eigentliche Machen erworben werden, Locke sieht dies mehr als Mittel zur Erziehung, um für das praktische Leben nützlich zu machen. Sie sind Teil seines Bildungsideals für einen englischen Gentleman, wie er detailliert in seinem Werk „Gedanken über Erziehung" beschreibt. Mit seinem Bezug zu grossen Männern des Altertums, die neben den Staatsgeschäften auch handwerkliche Tätigkeiten verrichteten, gibt er dem manuellen, alltäglichen Tun noch eine zusätzliche Wertigkeit.[5] Diese neue Wertschätzung führt laut Hanna Arendt dazu, dass handwerkliches Arbeiten als Teil des Erziehungsprozesses wieder zu mehr Ansehen kam.[6]

Allgemeingültige Grundsätze der Erziehung finden sich auch in Jean-Jacques Rousseaus Buch „Emile ou De l'education"[7]. Darin lernt der Protagonist Emil nicht aus Büchern, sondern eignet sich mit seinen Sinnen durch eigene Erfahrungen und Selbstständigkeit sein Wissen an. Sein erlerntes Handwerk dient ihm dabei als Ausgleich zur geistigen Tätigkeit und intellektuellen Erziehung. Er lernt durch seine Erfahrung und nicht durch unverstandene, theoretische Worte.[8]

Die handwerkliche Betätigung als Teil der Ausbildung findet sich in Ausbildungsströmungen bis ins 20. Jahrhundert in Europa wieder. Zu nennen sind hier besonders die Vorreiter Pestalozzi und Fröbel mit ihren Ausbildungsansätzen. Während Johann Heinrich Pestalozzi seine Schüler handwerklich arbeiten lässt, um sie so zur Selbstständigkeit anzuregen,[9] sieht Friedrich Fröbel im manuellen Tun die Gestaltung des Geistes und entwickelt dafür Spieltechniken und den heutigen Kindergarten.[10] Beide eint der Fokus auf ganzheitliches Zusammenspiel von handwerklichem

Tun und geistigen Überlegungen, um dadurch eigenes Lernen zu erreichen. Beeinflusst von Fröbels Pädagogik findet sich diese Bestrebung, Praxis in die Architekturlehre zu integrieren, auch bei Frank Lloyd Wright wieder, der seine Schüler am Bau von Taliesin handwerklich beteiligte.[11]

Making

1:1-Projekte in der Architekturausbildung sensibilisieren für die Einheit von Entwerfen-Konstruieren-Bauen. Dies ermöglicht den Studierenden, die Rolle als Koordinator, Entwerfer, Handwerker und Bauarbeiter in einem zu erfahren. Der Computer kommt dabei als Werkzeug zum Einsatz, in Sinne von Louis Kahn, der auf einer Podiumsdiskussion 1968 in Yale bemerkte, dass das schöpferische Fundament der Architektur das Entwerfen und Entwickeln ist und dieses nicht vom Computer übernommen werden soll.[12]

In dieser aktiven Lernumgebung ist das Erlernen der manuellen handwerklichen Fähigkeiten im Sinne von John Locke durch den Fokus auf das Sammeln von eigener Erfahrung zu verstehen. Auch stehen für die Studierenden das Lösen und Entwickeln von konstruktiven Details, die Einheit von Konstruktion und Gestalt im Zentrum der Tätigkeit. Die Zusammenarbeit erfolgte beim Bau der Modellwerkstatt durch die direkte Kooperation mit den Handwerksbetrieben und ihren Mitarbeitern. Diese gelebte Teamarbeit zwischen Handwerkern und Studierenden hebt den Bau der Modellwerkstatt von anderen 1:1-Projekten ab und wurde von den Studierenden und Handwerksbetrieben sehr geschätzt.

Modellwerkstatt

Der Ursprung für den Entwurfs- und Realisierungsprozess der Modellwerkstatt an der Universität Liechtenstein war die Notwendigkeit, neue Räumlichkeiten für die handwerklichen Modellbautätigkeiten unserer Architekturstudierenden zu schaffen, da die vorhandenen Räumlichkeiten in die Jahre gekommen waren und ein Neubau erforderlich war.

Beim Bau der Modellwerkstatt setzten wir das Material Holz als treibende Kraft beim Entwerfen und bei der anschliessenden handwerklichen Umsetzung ein. Der Startpunkt des Entwurfsprozesses war ein fünftägiger Workshop im Rahmen des Erasmus+-Programmes „Crafting the Façade", das von der Universität Liechtenstein koordiniert und mit der Academie van Bouwkunst, Amsterdam, und der Mackintosh School of Architecture, Glasgow, während drei Jahren durchgeführt wurde. Acht Tragstrukturen wurden in international gemischten Studierendenteams entwickelt und im Massstab 1:1 vor Ort gebaut und aufgerichtet. Die Aussenlinie der Tragstrukturen wurde vorgegeben, da die tunnelförmige Form die bestehenden baurechtlichen Bestimmungen am dafür vorgesehenen Platz hinter dem bestehenden Gebäude am besten erfüllte. Nach einer kurzen Entwurfsphase mit Modellen im Massstab 1:10 entschieden sich die Teams für ein klares konstruktives Konzept, das in zwei Tagen im Massstab 1:1 als Segment aufgebaut wurde. Als Baumaterial standen Stäbe von 10 × 10 cm und Bretter von 10 × 2 cm zur Auswahl. Die acht Segmente wurden zum Abschluss auf einem Holzpodest aneinandergereiht und bildeten zusammen als experimentelles Mock-up mit heterogener Struktur einen ersten Eindruck der zukünftigen Modellwerkstatt.

Im kommenden Semester entwickelten die zwei Entwurfsstudios von Urs Meister und Carmen Rist-Stadelmann aus diesen acht Tragstrukturen in einem nächsten Schritt vier baubare Strukturen. In einem lebendigen Zusammenspiel von Kopf und Hand in Form von Skizzen und 1:1-Tests entwarfen die Studierenden diese Strukturen weiter und bauten sie als Prototypen im Massstab 1:1. Eine kleine Jury aus Dozierenden und Studierenden wählte aus den vier Tragstrukturen schliesslich die Struktur aus, die für den Bau der Modellwerkstatt realisiert werden sollte. Die entscheidenden Auswahlkriterien für diese Struktur waren einerseits, dass die Tragstruktur konstruktiv sowohl Wand als auch Decke im tektonischen Sinne bildet und aus den Eigenschaften des Materials heraus entwickelt wurde. Andererseits sollte die Struktur von den Studierenden ohne Spezialisten und ohne grossen Computeraufwand selbst zu realisieren sein, um damit den didaktisch geforderten handwerklichen Aspekt einzulösen.

Für den Fertigungsprozess der Tragstruktur bauten die Studierenden in der Werkstatthalle der Zimmerei Frommelt Lehren, in welche die schmalen und langen Holzbretter eingefügt, verbunden und abschliessend zu Segmentbögen von einem Meter Breite fixiert wurden. Dazu wurden die Bretter so dünn wie möglich gehobelt, damit sie der gewünschten Biegung noch standhalten konnten und dabei nicht zerbrachen, ein empirischer Prozess, in dem die richtige Dimension erst gefunden werden musste. Der Boden wurde ebenfalls mit gebogenen Brettern unterspannt und elementiert. Nach einer Woche Vorfertigung in der Werkstatt wurden sämtliche Elemente der Tragstruktur zur Universität transportiert und in wenigen Stunden zu einem eindrücklichen Gerippe zusammenmontiert, das bereits sowohl den feingliedrigen Innenraum wie auch die markante Aussenform der Modellwerkstatt preisgab. In einem wochenlangen Ausbauprozess wurden im Team die gedämmte Aussenhülle und das hinterlüftete Schindeldach aufgebaut, die Glasfronten und Eingangstüren errichtet und schliesslich der Hartholzboden gelegt. Für die Sanitär-, Elektro- und Lüftungsinstallationen und den Einbau des Holzpelletofens wurden Installateure beigezogen.

Die Realisierung der Modellbauwerkstatt war ein rollender Prozess, in dem die Studierenden in verschiedenen Teams unterschiedliche konstruktive Bereiche wie z. B. die Positionierung und den Bau der Tür- und Fensterelemente oder den Anschluss der Oberlichtfenster an die Tragstruktur lösten. Um die Fertigstellung innerhalb des Entwurfssemesters zu erreichen, erfolgte das Planen und Bauen parallel im Team. Mit gemeinsamen Präsentationen wurde das Projekt im Sinne der Aktionsforschung beobachtet, reflektiert und weiterentwickelt. Am Modell im Massstab 1:10, das eine Studierendengruppe während des Bauprozesses realisierte, konnten sämtliche Entscheidungen überprüft werden, um sie anschliessend vor Ort im Massstab 1:1 zu bauen. Somit entstand ein spannendes Wechselspiel von Theorie und Praxis anhand des Modells und des Baus in Realität, von dem die Studierenden laut ihren eigenen Aussagen stark profitieren konnten. Durch diese Art von Herstellungsprozess trat die individuelle Autorenschaft in den Hintergrund und liess die Vielzahl von gestalterischen Entscheidungen aller Mitwirkenden zu einem neuen Ganzen verschmelzen.

Der Bauprozess war eine Teamarbeit von 61 Studierenden, drei Dozierenden und fünf Zimmermännern. Nach 15 Wochen intensiven Bauens, Konstruierens und Entwerfens war die Modellwerkstatt am Semesterende so weit fertig, dass sie feierlich eröffnet werden konnte. Die letzten noch abschliessenden Arbeiten und das Umsiedeln der Maschinen erfolgten während der Sommerferien, sodass die Werkstatt im September 2017 erstmals in Betrieb gehen konnte.

Every time man uses his know-how / *His experience increases* / *And his intellectual advantages* / *Automatically increases.* / *Because of its conservation* / *Energy cannot decrease.* / *Know-how can only increase.*

Buckminster Fuller[1]

Today's differentiation, specialisation and mechanisation of professional activities emerged at the beginning of the industrial age and during its subsequent development: from the separation of craft and art, to the division of the art of construction into a world of designed architecture and calculated engineering, to the replacement of labour through current digital innovations. According to László Moholy-Nagy, this results in a state of affairs in educational culture that engenders a 'compartmentalised person' whose holistic development is thereby inhibited.[2] For Juhani Pallasmaa, this increase in specialisation fragments architecture and architectural identity as well as the working process, and ultimately weakens the built product. He criticises the corresponding increase in distance between the practical and the intellectual, between the studio and the construction site. For Pallasmaa, the architects of today draw up their plans in the secure isolation of the studio. They act more like advocates, who work on cases from the office and thus no longer engage with and discover the material nor incorporate the physical processes of making in their deliberations.[3] This separation is facilitated through the advance of computers and the accompanying digitalisation that continues to transform these traditional processes. Therefore it is no surprise that there is currently a pronounced desire to integrate various facets of practice into architectural education, in order to give more space back to hands-on processes.

Stimuli for making

The endeavour to integrate manual work as a practice-oriented component of educational training in order to provide solid preparation for the students' future professional lives is not solely a tendency of our current age and should not, as a look at the history of pedagogy reveals, be viewed in isolation.

One of the first to recognise the educational value of skilled manual work was the Englishman John Locke.[4] From his perspective, manual activity produces a healthy mind in a healthy body. Handicraft skills need not be acquired for the act of making itself; rather, he sees them more as a means of education that makes one useful for practical life. They are part of his educational ideals for an English gentleman, which he describes in detail in his work, *Some Thoughts Concerning Education*. By drawing a connection to the great men of the ancient world—who, in addition to conducting state business also engaged in manual work—he bestows additional value upon manual, everyday action.[5] According to Hanna Arendt, this new appreciation has meant that manual work has once again gained more respect as a component of the educational process.[6]

Universally valid principles of education are also found in Jean Jacques Rousseau's book, *Émile, ou de l'education* (*Emile, or On Education*).[7] In this book, the protagonist Emil not only learns from books, but also acquires knowledge by using his own senses, through self-reliance and his own experiences. The skilled craft he acquired thus serves to counterbalance mental activity and intellectual education. He learns through experience and not through obscure, theoretical words.[8]

Manual activity as a component of educational training is again found in pedagogical movements in Europe extending into the 20th century. Of particular importance here are the pioneers Pestalozzi and Fröbel, along with their pedagogical approaches. While Johann Heinrich Pestalozzi has his students do manual work in order to foster their self-reliance,[9] Friedrich Fröbel sees manual activity as a means to form the mind and thus develops techniques of play and the contemporary nursery school.[10] Both are united by their focus on the holistic interplay of handicraft and intellectual reflection in order to achieve self-directed learning. Under the influence of Fröbel's pedagogy, Frank Lloyd Wright also joined in the efforts to integrate practice into architectural education by involving his students in the physical act of building Taliesin.[11]

Making

Undertaking full-scale projects in architectural education raise awareness of the unity of designing, developing and building. This allows students to simultaneously explore the roles of coordinator, designer, craftsperson and construction worker. Computers are used solely as a tool, in the spirit of Louis Kahn's remarks in a 1968 panel discussion at Yale, where he noted that the creative foundation of architecture is design and development, and that this should not be taken over by a computer.[12]

In this environment of active learning, the acquisition of skills in a manual craft is to be understood in the Lockean sense of focusing on the accumulating of personal experience. For the students, the resolution and development of construction details as well as the unity of construction and design are also the focus of their work. The collaborative effort of building the model workshop took place in direct cooperation with the building trade firms and their personnel. This lived experience of teamwork among craftspeople and students distinguishes the construction of the model workshop from other life-size projects and was highly valued by the students and the building trade firms.

Model workshop

The process of designing and building the model workshop at the University of Liechtenstein originated from the need for new facilities to enable the architecture students to make models by hand, since the existing facilities had become outdated over time and needed to be replaced by a new building.

For building the model workshop, the timber material served as the driving force behind our design and in the ensuing task of carrying out the work by hand. The starting point for the design process was a five-day workshop, held as part of the Erasmus+ programme 'Crafting the Façade', that was coordinated by the University of Liechtenstein and conducted over a period of three years with the Amsterdam Academy of Architecture and the Mackintosh School of Architecture. Eight load-bearing structures were developed by internationally mixed teams of students and then assembled and erected on site at full scale. The outer profile of the load-bearing structures was a given, since the tunnel-shaped form best complied with the applicable building regulations for the designated site behind the existing building. Following a brief design phase with models at 1:10 scale, each of the teams decided on a clear constructional concept that was executed as a full-scale segment in just two days. The building materials available to choose from were 10 × 10 cm posts / rails and 10 × 2 cm boards. On completion, the eight different segments were aligned in row on a wooden platform to form an experimental mock-up with a heterogeneous structure that offered a first impression of the future model workshop.

In the following semester, the two design studios led by Urs Meister and Carmen Rist-Stadelmann took the next step and developed four buildable constructions from these eight load-bearing structures. Through a lively interplay between mind and hand in the form of sketches and full-scale trials, the students developed these structures further and built them as prototypes at full scale. From these four load-bearing structures, a small jury of lecturers and students ultimately chose one for use to build the future model workshop. The decisive criteria for selecting this structure were, on the one hand, that the load-bearing structure constructively forms both wall and ceiling and is developed from the material's properties. On the other hand, the students should be able to build the structure themselves, without specialists and with only minimal use of computers, and in this way satisfy the craft aspect demanded by the didactic concept.

To fabricate the load-bearing structure, the students built jigs inside the Frommelt carpentry shop, into which the narrow and long wooden boards were inserted, joined and finally assembled into one-metre-wide segmental arches. In addition, the boards were planed as thin as possible so they could withstand imposing the desired curvature without breaking—necessitating an empirical process in which the right dimension first had to be found. The floor was likewise braced from below with curved boards and fabricated in modules. Following a week of prefabrication in the workshop, all elements of the load-bearing structure were transported to the university and assembled in a few hours to form an impressive skeleton that already revealed the delicately refined interior space as well as the striking external shape of the workshop building. During the weeks-long process of fitting out the building, the team affixed the insulated outer skin and the ventilated shingled roof, erected the glass fronts and entry doors, and lastly laid the hardwood floor. Specialists were brought in to install the sanitary, electrical and ventilation systems as well as the wood pellet furnace.

The realisation of the model-building workshop was a rolling process, in which the students in the various teams resolved diverse construction problems such as the positioning and fabrication of the door and window elements as well as the juncture between the skylights and the load-bearing structure. In order to complete the project during the design semester, planning and building were carried out in parallel by the teams. Group presentations were used to monitor, reflect upon and further develop the project in the spirit of action research. Using a model at 1:10 scale, which a group of students made while the construction process was ongoing, all decisions could be checked first and then built on site at full scale. This made for an exciting interplay between theory and practice on the basis of the model and the real-world construction, from which, according to their own statements, the students benefited greatly. Through this kind of production process, individual authorship receded to the background and allowed the myriad design decisions of all the participants to fuse into a new whole.

The building process was conducted as a team project with 61 students, 3 lecturers and 5 carpenters. After 15 weeks of intensive building, detailing and designing, the model workshop was sufficiently complete at the end of the semester for it to be ceremonially inaugurated. The final remaining work and installation of the machinery took place during the summer break, thus allowing the workshop to begin operation in September 2017.

Experimentelle Prototypen
Experimental Prototypes

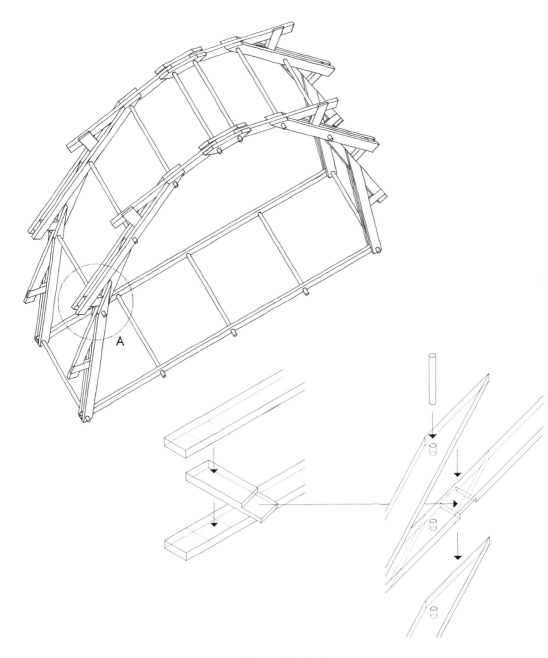

Rocco Cutieri

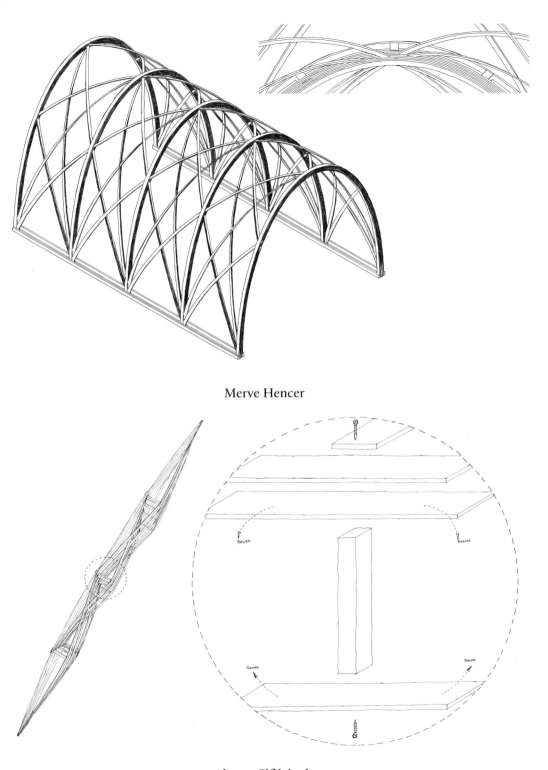

Merve Hencer

Ahmet Cifticioglu

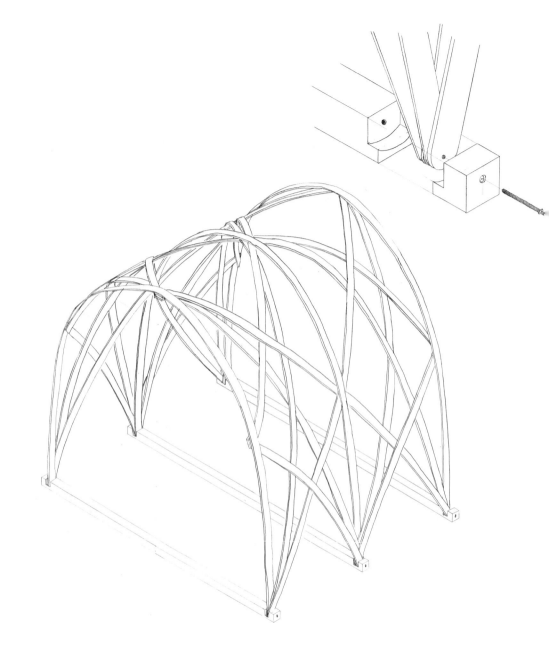

Lennon Lee Hartmann

Experimentelle Prototypen Experimental Prototypes

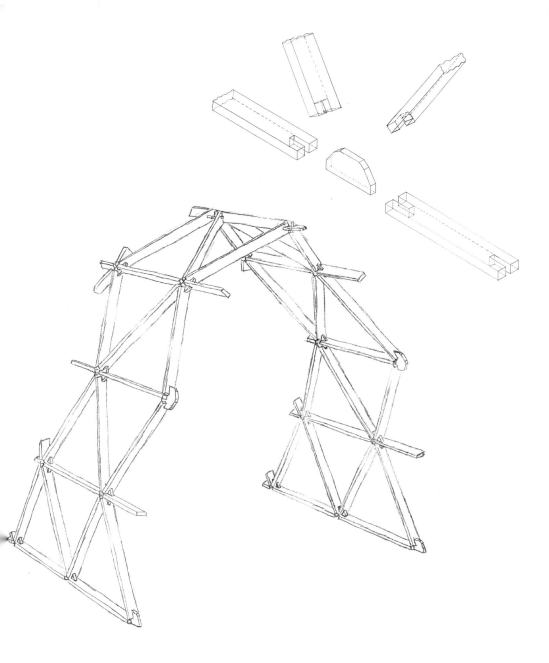

Susanne Brandt

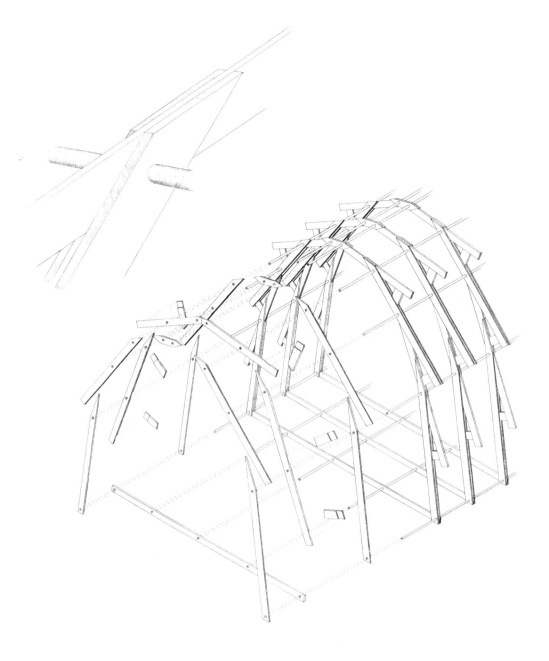

Seraina Bernegget

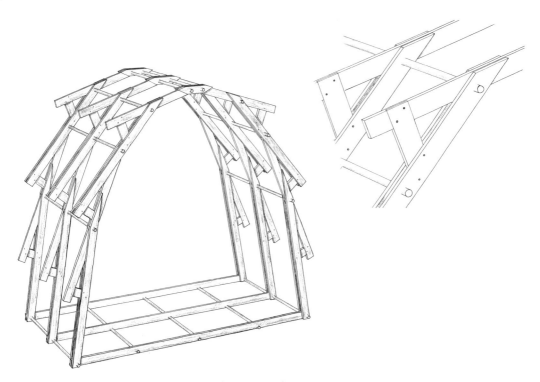

Andreas Brandstetter

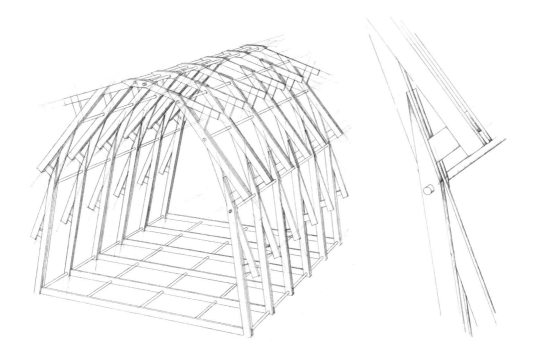

Ruben De Sá

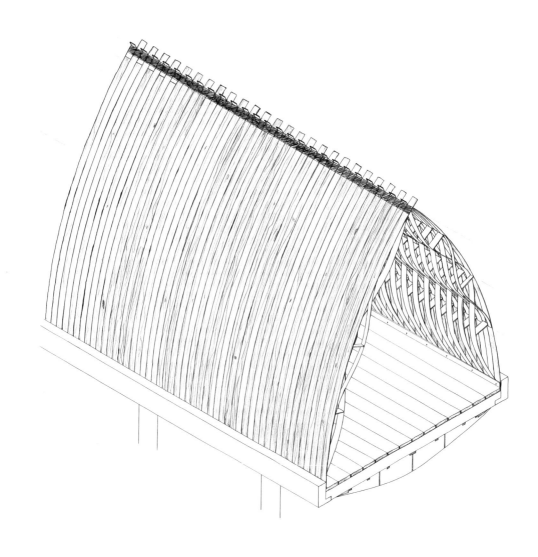

Marcella Zauner

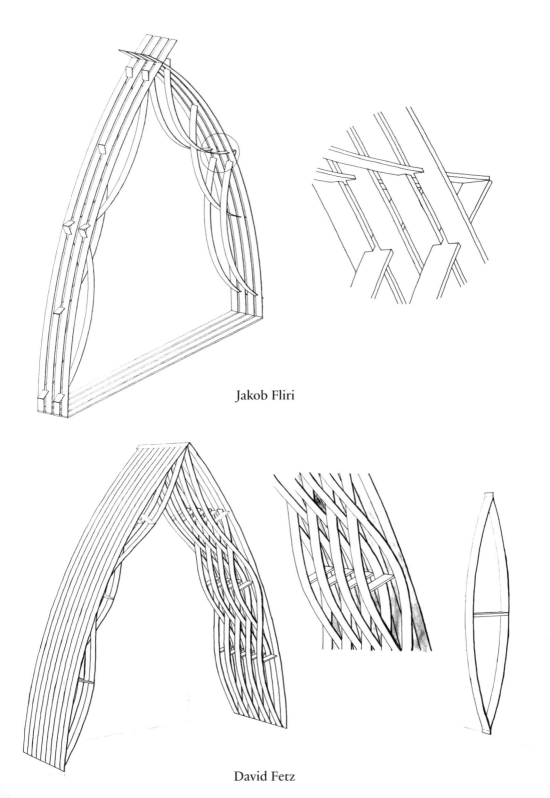

Jakob Fliri

David Fetz

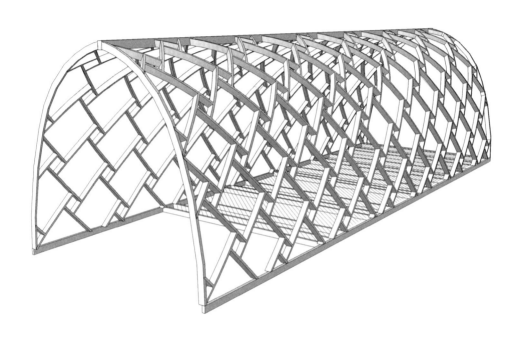

Christoph Ammer, Dionys Rieder

Experimentelle Prototypen Experimental Prototypes

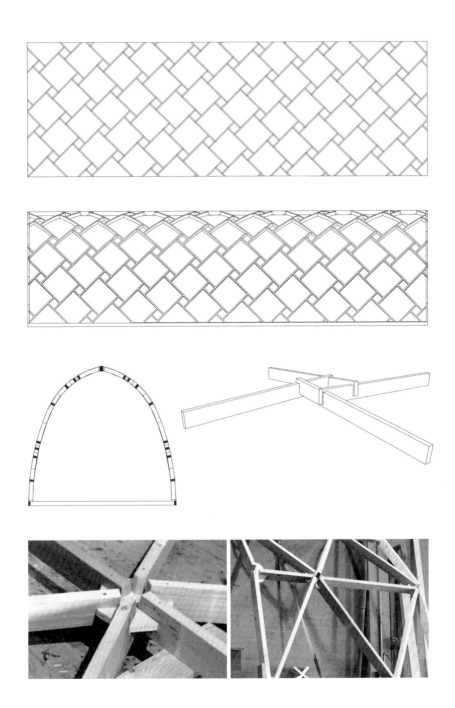

Fabio Schober, Livia Herle

Experimentelle Prototypen Experimental Prototypes

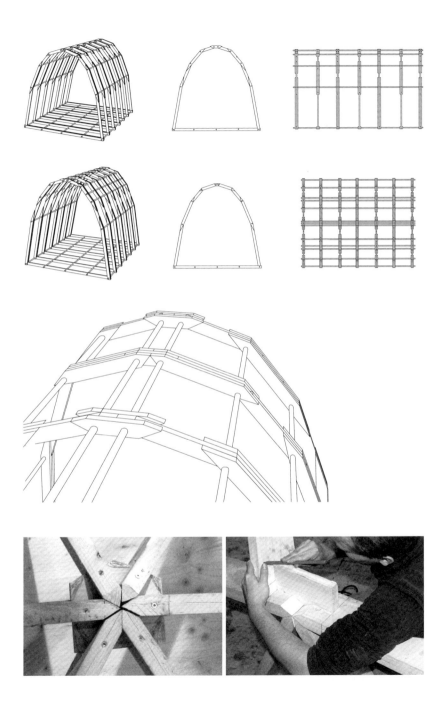

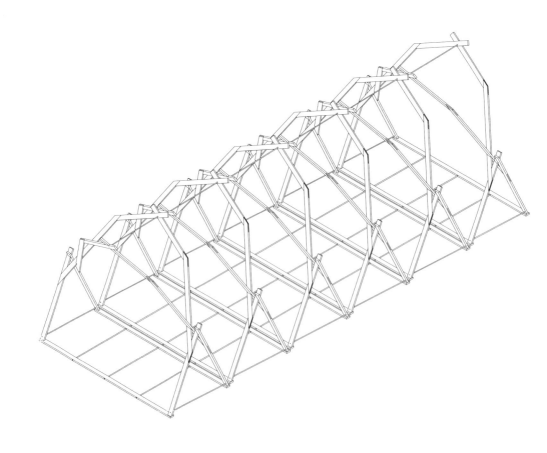

Albert Paletta, Alexander Meissner

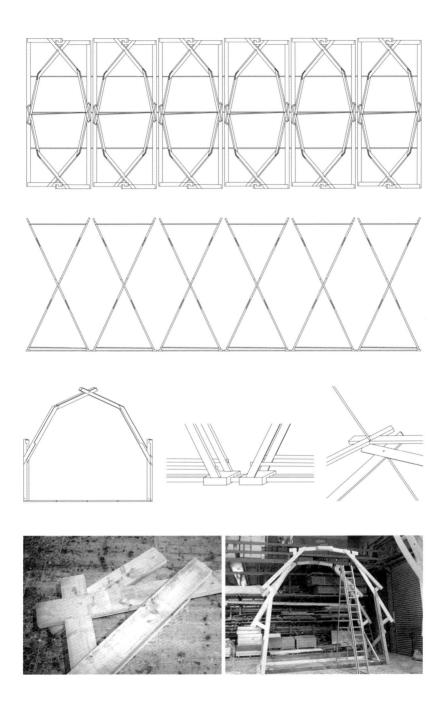

Philipp Althammer, Lino Nägele

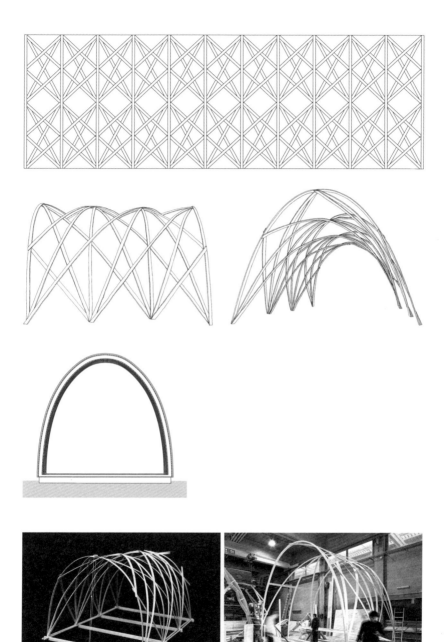

95

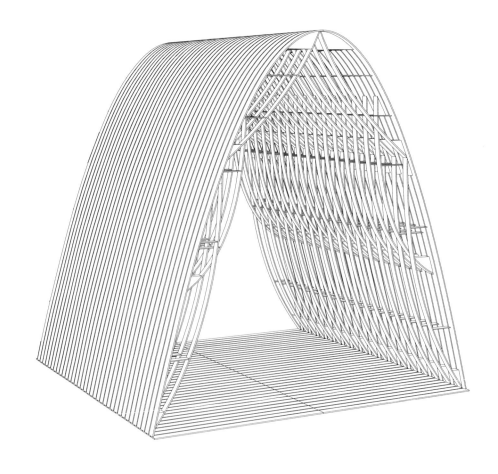

Kerstin Thurnher, Viviane Göbel

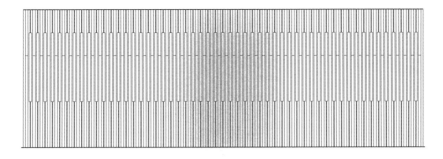
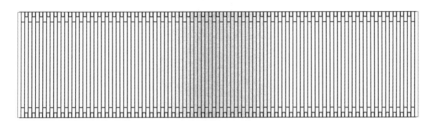
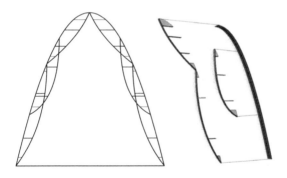

Die Urhütte
The Primitive Hut

Machiel Spaan

Die Ursprünge der Architektur liegen im Bedürfnis des Menschen, sich vor Witterungseinflüssen und Schädlingen zu schützen, schreibt der Architekt Gottfried Semper in seinem Hauptwerk „Der Stil in den technischen und tektonischen Künsten oder praktische Ästhetik." Seine *Vier Elemente der Architektur* formen diesen Schutz: Boden, Wand und Dach schirmen uns vor äusseren Einflüssen ab, die Feuerstelle spendet Wärme. Mit jedem Element verbindet Semper ein Material: Wand mit Textil, Dach mit Holz, Boden mit Stein, Feuerstelle mit Keramik. Wir ernten diese Materialien von der Natur und bauen daraus unser Haus. Indem wir sie nach den Gesetzen der Natur einsetzen, entsteht eine vom Menschen geformte Architektur, die ihrerseits wiederum Teil der Natur wird.

Ich erinnere mich an unsere erste Hütte, die wir aus Materialien bauten, die wir auf dem Feld hinter unserem Haus fanden. Wir ebneten den Boden, steckten eine Reihe von Rundpfählen in die Erde und verbanden sie mit Brettern, die wir von einer nahe gelegenen Baustelle geborgen hatten. Für den Boden verwendeten wir Platten, die von einem ehemaligen Gehsteig stammten. Aus Sperrholz und Wellblechplatten von derselben Baustelle bauten wir die Wände, die wir zwischen den Pfählen befestigten. In eines der Bleche sägten wir ein grosses Loch, damit wir hinein- und hinausgehen konnten. Mit dem ausgesägten Stück konnten wir das Loch schliessen. Für das Dach benutzten wir Bretter, die auf die Seite gedreht und in einem leichten Winkel angebracht wurden. Darauf legten wir mit schwarzem Bauplastik überzogene Holzbretter, die wir an den Seiten mit Holzlatten und Nägeln befestigten. Schlitze zwischen dem Dach und den Wänden liessen Licht eindringen. Im Inneren stellten wir eine Feuerstelle her, indem wir Steine aus dem Feld aufstapelten. Den Rauch leiteten wir mit einem auf der Strasse gefundenen Rohr durch die Wand. Kaum war die Hütte fertig, überstanden wir darin einen Regenschauer.

Im Gegensatz zur Urhütte von Laugier, die mit direkt aus dem Wald entnommenen Ästen gebaut wurde, ist Sempers Hütte aus vorab bearbeiteten Komponenten zusammengesetzt. Ein stabiler *schwebender* Boden auf Beinen, Stützen, Dachbalken mit vorbereiteten Verbindungen, ein Dach aus Holzschindeln, Wände aus gewebtem Textil. Damit sich die natürlichen Materialien (Lehm, Holz, Stein, Baumwolle, Flechtwerk) für den Zusammenbau eignen, müssen sie zunächst bearbeitet werden. Man könnte behaupten, dass der erste Schritt zur Architektur die Verarbeitung von Materialien zu Bauteilen ist. Dafür sind ein Arbeitsplatz und Werkzeuge hilfreich. Und dies ist der Ursprung der Werkstatt, die vor der gebauten Architektur kam. Die Werkstatt ist der Ort, an dem wir den Baumstamm zu Balken sägen, rohes Gestein zu stapelbaren Steinen schneiden und Ton zu Platten oder Dachziegeln formen.

Eine gute Werkstatt beginnt mit einem ebenen und stabilen Boden – der *Form*, wie Semper sie nennt. Auf ihm kann das zu bearbeitende Material sicher platziert werden. Ein Hebezeug und ein Arbeitstisch können stabil auf dem Boden stehen. Und auch der Handwerker muss fest auf seinen Füssen stehen. Das Dach schützt die Materialien und den Handwerker vor Sonne, Wind und Regen. Wände umschliessen das Atelier und bieten Schutz. Grosse Öffnungen in den Wänden ermöglichen den Transport grosser Gegenstände nach innen und aussen und sorgen für ausreichend Tageslicht zum Arbeiten im Inneren.

Die ersten Ideen für die Gestaltung der neuen Modellwerkstatt in Vaduz entstanden während eines Workshops mit Studierenden aus den Niederlanden, Norwegen und Liechtenstein. Aus den von den Studierenden selbst gefertigten Holzverbindungen wurden mehrere Dachbinder konstruiert, zuerst in kleinem Massstab und dann in vollem Massstab. Das Ergebnis des Workshops war eine Serie von acht einzigartigen Fachwerkbindern, die auf dem Gelände der zukünftigen Modellwerkstatt aufgestellt wurden. Einer dieser Dachbinder bildete den Ausgangspunkt für den Folgeprozess. Der Binder besteht aus zwei dünnen Holzbrettern, die ineinander verwoben sind. Kurze Querlatten zwischen den Brettern machten den Binder zu einer starken Struktur. Im folgenden Jahr arbeiteten die Studierenden den Entwurf an der Universität Liechtenstein aus und bauten das Gebäude tatsächlich.

Der Bau begann mit der Herstellung einer stabilen Basis. Grosse Zementrohre, die mit Beton ausgegossen wurden, hoben den Werkstattboden etwa 30 Zentimeter über den Grund an, um Wasser und Ungeziefer fernzuhalten. Der Boden wurde nivelliert und diente als stabile Basis für das Gebäude. Auf diesem waagerechten Boden wurde konstruiert und gebaut. Ein perfekt ebener Boden war für die künftige Modellwerkstatt auch entscheidend, denn er dient als Wasserwaage, mit der alle Objekte auf die Erde bezogen werden konnten. Senkrechte Ecken waren für ein gutes Ergebnis unerlässlich. Schliesslich fungierte der Boden auch als Podium, als eine über die Natur erhobene Schalung, auf der die Produkte des Ateliers präsentiert werden konnten. Der Boden wurde zu einem der Handwerkskunst gewidmeten Altar. Am Eingang betonen zwei Stufen aus Naturstein das über der Landschaft schwebende Podium.

Der Boden erfüllt in diesem Fall verschiedene Funktionen. Während der Bauphase diente er als Konstruktionsboden für das Gebäude. Nach Beendigung des Baus wurde er zum Arbeitsboden und für die Nutzung als Atelier nivelliert. Schliesslich wird er zu einem Podium für die Ausstellung von Modellen und Mock-ups und zu einem Podium für die Modellwerkstatt selbst.

Sobald der Boden fertig war, konnte der Raum überdacht werden. Die leichten Dachbinder ähneln einer Zeltstruktur. Nach der Montage der vorgefertigten Bogenelemente setzten die Studierenden die Dachschalung ein und belegten die Dachhaut mit Holzschindeln. Danach war die

Baustelle überdacht, geschützt vor Wind und Regen, und der Innenausbau konnte im Trockenen erfolgen. Die gewählte Form der Holzkonstruktion ist eine Kreuzung aus Wand und Dach. Die gebogenen Wände laufen nach oben hin zusammen. Oder, anders ausgedrückt, das gebogene Dach endet am Boden. Diese zugespitzte Dach- und Wandform lässt den Schnee vom Gebäude abrutschen. Ein Oberlicht an der Spitze, wo sich die gebogenen Binder treffen, lässt Licht tief in das Gebäude eindringen. Die Vorder- und die Rückseite der Modellwerkstatt sind komplett aus Glas. Nicht nur Licht und Luft, sondern auch Baumaterialien und Produkte können hier ungehindert hineingelangen.

Die Leichtbaustruktur verleiht der Modellwerkstatt den Eindruck von Feinheit, Luftigkeit und Freiheit. Das Gebäude sitzt sanft an seinem Ort. Die verglasten Endfassaden zeigen das Handwerk gegen aussen. Studierende gehen ein und aus, tragen Teile von Modellen, Mock-ups und Zeichnungen. Die Modellwerkstatt ist kein geschlossener Raum, sondern ein offener Ort des Lernens, an dem Ideen sichtbar sind und gezeigt werden. Ein Ort der Inspiration für den Austausch von Wissen und Handfertigkeit. Ein Ort, an dem man lernt, indem man zuschaut und macht.

Der Entwurf und die Struktur begannen im Studio, wurden aber nach und nach zur Architektur. Studio und Architektur sind eng miteinander verbunden. Der Entwurf der Holzbinder ergab sich aus der Verbindung, der Fuge, den gebogenen Holzbrettern, die sich aneinanderschmiegen. Der Entwurf spiegelt perfekt Sempers Idee wider, dass Architektur mit Materialien beginnt, die vor Ort gefunden werden, und mit Techniken, die durch die Verarbeitung dieser Materialien entdeckt werden. Der kreative Prozess der Hütte folgt diesem Gedankengang. Unerfahrene Studierende entwickelten Holzverbindungen, die ein Jahr später in einer faszinierenden Gebäudestruktur resultierten.

Sempers vier Elemente der Architektur sind in der fertigen Modellwerkstatt sichtbar präsent. Der Boden ist das prominenteste Element. Er bildet die Basis sowohl für die Baustelle als auch für die Modellwerkstatt selbst. Die Elemente Wand und Dach sind vereint durch die Techniken des Flechtens und der Holzbearbeitung, die laut Semper mit dem Material korrespondieren. Die Binderkonstruktion wurde mit schlanken

Holzbrettern zusammenfügt und mit Querlatten verflochten. Die Elemente wurden in der Werkhalle der Zimmerei vorbereitet und auf dem Arbeitsboden zusammengesetzt. Das vierte Element, die Feuerstelle, hat die Form eines Kamins und eines Holzofens, der in der Mitte des Raumes platziert ist und in dem Holzabfälle und Sägespäne in Wärme umgewandelt werden.

Schliesslich ist die Modellwerkstatt in Vaduz nicht nur ein Ort, an dem Studierende arbeiten und lernen, sondern auch das Ergebnis eines Studierendenworkshops. Das Gebäude ist sowohl das Ergebnis der kreativen Arbeit als auch eine Kraft, die die Kreativität antreibt. Es zeigt, dass Material, Technik und Handwerk auf allen Ebenen miteinander verwoben sind. Materialien lassen sich nach ihren eigenen Gesetzen verarbeiten, unabhängig von Stil und Form.

Wenn die Urhütte von Semper wieder gebaut würde, stünde sie in Vaduz.

The origins of architecture lie in the need to protect ourselves from inclement weather conditions and pests, writes architect Gottfried Semper in his magnum opus *Style in the Technical and Tectonic Arts; or, Practical Aesthetics*. His four elements of architecture constitute this protection. The floor, wall and roof shield us from external influences, and the hearth provides warmth. To each element Semper links a material: wall and textile, roof and wood, floor and stone, hearth and ceramics. We harvest these materials from nature and use them to construct our 'house'. Applying them according to the laws of nature results in an architecture, shaped by man, which in turn also becomes part of nature.

I remember our first hut, constructed from materials found in the field behind our house. We levelled the ground, inserted a number of round stakes into the soil and connected them with planks salvaged from a nearby construction site. For the floor, we used slabs taken from what used to be a sidewalk. We built up the walls from plywood and sheets of corrugated iron, also taken from the construction site, which we fixed between the stakes. We sawed a big hole in one of the sheets so we could go in and out. We could close the hole with the piece we had sawn off. For the roof, we used planks turned on their sides and placed at a slight angle. On top of them we arranged timber planks covered in black agricultural plastic that we fixed at the sides using timber slats and nails. Slits that appeared between the roof and walls allowed light to seep in. Inside, we created a hearth by stacking stones taken from the field. We channelled the smoke through the wall using a pipe found on the street. The hut was finished as soon as we survived a rain shower.

In contrast to the primitive hut of Laugier, which is constructed of branches taken directly from the forest, Semper's hut is assembled from components processed in advance. A stable 'floating' floor on legs, plus columns, roof beams with prepared connections, roofing of timber shingles, and walls of woven textile. To make the natural materials (clay, wood, stone, cotton, wickerwork, etc.) suitable for construction, they first need to be processed. You could argue that the first step towards architecture is the processing of materials into building components. For this, a workplace and tools are helpful. And this is the origin of the work studio, which came before built architecture. The studio is where we saw the tree trunk into beams, cut rough stone into stackable bricks, and shape clay into panels or roof tiles.

A good work studio starts with a level and strong floor — the 'mould' as Semper calls it. The material to be processed can be placed securely on it. A hoist and worktable can stand firmly on the floor. And the craftsman must also stand firmly on his feet. The roof protects the materials and the craftsman from the sun, wind and rain. Walls enclose the studio and provide protection. Large openings in the walls make it possible to transport big objects inside and outside and ensure sufficient daylight for work inside.

The first ideas for the design of the new work studio in Vaduz surfaced during a workshop with students from the Netherlands, Norway and Liechtenstein. A number of trusses were constructed using timber joints created by the students themselves, first at a small scale and then at full scale. The workshop resulted in a series of twelve unique trusses that were temporarily positioned on the site of the future studio. One of these trusses provided the point of departure for the follow-up process. The truss is composed of two thin wooden slats 'woven' into each other. A crossbeam between the slats makes the truss a strong structure. The following year, the students elaborated on the design at the University of Liechtenstein and actually constructed the building.

Construction began with making a stable base. Large segments of cement pipe filled with concrete elevated the floor some 30 centimetres above the rocky ground, thereby keeping water and pests out. The floor was made level and served as a stable base for the building. Making and constructing would take place on this horizontal floor. A perfectly level floor was also crucial for the future studio, for it would act as a measurement gauge by which all objects could be related to the earth. Right-angled corners were essential for a good result.

Finally, the floor also functioned as a podium, a 'mould', elevated above nature, where products from the studio could be presented. The floor became an altar dedicated to craftsmanship. Two blocks of natural stone form steps at the entrance, thus emphasising the podium floating above the landscape. The floor in this case performs various functions. During construction it served as a platform for constructing the building. After the construction work was completed, it became a work floor and was levelled for studio use. Finally, it becomes a podium for displaying models and mock-ups and a podium for the studio itself.

Once the floor was finished, the space could be 'roofed'. The lightweight trusses resemble a tent structure. After positioning the prefabricated curved components, the students placed the roof boarding and the timber roof tiles. The construction site was then covered, protected from wind and rain, and the interior could be completed under dry conditions.

The chosen form of the timber structure is a cross between a wall and a roof. The curved walls converge at the top. Or, put another way, the curved roof ends at the floor. This pointed roof and wall shape lets snow slide off the building. A roof light at the top where the curved trusses meet allows daylight to penetrate deep into the building. The front and rear of the studio are made entirely of glass. Not only light and air but also construction materials and products enter and exit here unimpeded.

The lightweight structure lends the studio a sense of lightness, airiness and freedom. The building sits gently on its site. The glazed ends display the craftsmanship to the world outside. Students walk in and out, carrying parts of models, mock-ups and drawings. The studio is not a closed space but an open place of learning where ideas are visible and displayed. A place of inspiration for sharing knowledge and craftsmanship. A place where you learn by looking around and doing.

The design and structure started as a studio but gradually became architecture. Studio and architecture are deeply connected to each other. The design of the timber truss resulted from the joint, the connection, the curved timber slats that weave past one another. It perfectly reflects Semper's idea that architecture starts with materials found locally and with techniques discovered through processing those materials. The creative process of the hut follows this line of thought. Unsuspecting students developed timber joints that resulted, one year later, in a fascinating building structure.

Semper's four elements of architecture are visibly present in the finished studio space. The floor is the most prominent element. It forms the basis for both the construction site and the studio. The elements of wall and roof are fused together using the techniques of woodworking and weaving that, according to Semper, correspond to their materials. The truss structure was assembled and woven with slender timber slats and round rods. The elements were prepared in the carpentry shop and assembled on the work floor. The fourth element, the hearth, takes the form of a chimney and wood burner placed in the middle of the space, where waste timber and sawdust are converted into heat.

Finally, the studio in Vaduz is not only a place where students work and learn, but also the result of a student workshop. The building is both the result of creative work *and* a force that drives creativity. It shows that materials, technology and craftsmanship are interwoven at all levels. Materials let themselves be processed according to their own laws, independently of style and shape.

If the primitive hut of Semper has been built again, it is standing in Vaduz.

Es hat uns niemand gesagt, was und wie wir das oder jenes machen. Wir probierten einfach und fanden es selber heraus. Das hat mir sehr gut gefallen.

Livia Herle
MSc Studierende

Nobody told us what and how to do this or that. We simply gave it a try and found out for ourselves. I liked that a lot.

Livia Herle
MSc student

Bauprozess Building Process

Bauprozess Building Process

Eine Werkstatt für die Universität
A Workshop for the University

Christoph Frommelt

Ingenieurskunst und Baukunst sollten wieder miteinander vereint funktionieren und nicht isoliert betrachtet werden. Die Projekte mit den Studierenden erzeugen die Möglichkeit, diese zwei Bereiche näher zusammenzubringen, verschiedene Ideen zu haben und sie gemeinsam zu realisieren. Erst in der Zusammenarbeit und im gemeinsamen Entwickeln kann Neues entstehen. Das ist eine wichtige Erfahrung fürs Leben und tut der Ausbildung gut.

Beim neuen Werkraum der Universität Liechtenstein durften wir einen neuen und experimentellen Weg beschreiten. In der Phase 1 arbeiteten wir im Rahmen eines Erasmus+-Projekts mit liechtensteinischen, niederländischen und schottischen Studierenden. Die in verschiedenen Gruppen aufgeteilten Studierenden erhielten die Aufgabe, eine Tragstruktur zu entwickeln und im Massstab 1:1 zu bauen. Diese Aufgabenstellung war für die Studierenden neu und sehr herausfordernd. Die Herausforderungen, Aufgaben und Lerneffekte in diesem speziellen Vorgehen lagen in folgenden Punkten:

— Entwicklung eines statischen Verständnisses
— Verschmelzung von statischer Struktur und Ästhetik
— Verbindungen von Stäben in Holz
— Arbeiten und entwickeln in einem heterogenen Team
— Handwerkliches Umsetzen eines Entwurfs

Aus den sehr überraschenden und speziellen Tragstrukturen wählte die Jury ein Projekt zur Umsetzung aus. In der Phase 2 bearbeiteten zehn Studierenden der Uni Liechtenstein, unterstützt von weiteren Studierenden, diese filigrane, unterspannte, räumliche Tragstruktur weiter. Der Weg führte von einer Konstruktion und Entwurfsidee über die Detailplanung bis hin zur Produktion des Werkraums. Ich durfte dieses experimentelle Projekt aus konstruktiver und handwerklicher Sicht begleiten und betreuen.

Umsetzung der Konstruktionsidee in einen Gesamtentwurf

Für die Aufgabe, aus der Tragstruktur eine Gesamtidee umzusetzen, waren folgende Schwerpunkte sehr wichtig:

— Das Grundprinzip und die Entwurfsregeln der Tragstruktur
  zu verstehen

- Lösungen im Entwurf zu finden, welche die Grundidee stärken
- Die Teams aus anderen Konstruktionsgruppen wieder für diese neue Idee zu gewinnen

Detailplanung

Bei der Detailplanung waren ca. zehn Studierenden in ca. fünf Zweiergruppen tätig und bekamen Teilaufgaben aus dem Gesamtprojekt. So ergaben sich folgende Themen und Lerneffekte mit vielen neuen und experimentellen Schwerpunkten:
- Konstruieren mit dem Rohstoff Holz
- Zusammenfügen der verschiedenen Details aus den Planungsgruppen in ein Ganzes (gemeinsamen Teamentscheid herbeiführen)
- Konstruieren auf Basis der Grundidee
- Produktions- und materialgerecht konstruieren
- Konstruktionsmodelle der Details anfertigen

Produktion

Die Haupttragstruktur produzierten die Studierenden bei uns in der Firma mit der spontanen Unterstützung des Leitungsteams und von Fachkräften aus unserer Produktion. Bei dieser Phase konnten viele Aspekte erlernt und erarbeitet werden:
- Ausführbarkeit der Details
- Handwerkliches Verständnis schulen
- Produktionsideen selber entwickeln und ausprobieren
- Organisation von Fachkräften mit verschiedenen Talenten

Montage

Die Montage ist bei jedem Handwerker und so auch bei den Studierenden die speziellste Phase. Es besteht die Ungewissheit, ob das Produzierte auch passt und zusammengefügt werden kann. Das Team erfährt mit eigenen Sinnen, ob das Entworfene und Konstruierte auch produzierbar und montierbar ist. Die Studierenden können sich auch fragen, ob das Bild, welches sie geistig entworfen haben, mit dem realen Bild übereinstimmt. Hinzu kommt die Freude beim Entstehen. Die Freude und der Eindruck werden noch viel stärker, wenn der gesamte Prozess in den Händen der Studierenden liegt.

Konstruktiv und statisch gesehen sind Strukturen entstanden, die nicht so einfach aus dem Ärmel geschüttelt werden, und auf die ein Ingenieur wahrscheinlich nie gekommen wäre. Architekturstudierende werden kreativer geschult und haben die Freiheit, unbeschwert an die Aufgabe herangehen zu können. Die Unwissenheit tut da gut, um neue Ideen zu entwickeln.

Zum Schluss möchte ich den Studierenden und Dozierenden gratulieren für dieses sehr schöne Holzbauprojekt. Aber vor allem kann man den Mut von Carmen und Urs nicht hoch genug schätzen. Den Mut, sich auf das Experiment einzulassen und den Weg mit den Studierenden zu gehen, von der Konstruktionsidee bis zum fertigen Bau. Als Fazit kann gesagt werden, dass für alle Beteiligten, also für die Studierenden, für das Projektteam und für mich, dies die beste Lösung ist: Lernen durch das Entwerfen, Detailplanen und Konstruieren mit Holz.

Engineering and architecture should once again work as one and not be viewed in isolation. These projects with the students create the opportunity to bring these two areas closer together, to have different ideas, and to jointly bring them to fruition. Only through collaboration and joint development can something new emerge. This is an important experience for life and is good for education.

For the new workshop space at the University of Liechtenstein, we were able to pursue a new and experimental path. In Phase 1, we worked with students from Liechtenstein, the Netherlands and Scotland as part of an Erasmus+ project. The students, who were divided into various groups, were given the task to develop a load-bearing structure and build it at full scale. This assignment was new and very challenging for the students. The challenges, responsibilities and learning effects in this specific approach resided in the following points:

— Development of a structural understanding
— Fusion of load-bearing structure and aesthetics
— Connections of wood members
— Working and developing in a heterogeneous team
— Handcrafted implementation of a design

From the very surprising and exceptional load-bearing structures, the jury selected one project for implementation. In Phase 2, ten students from the University of Liechtenstein, supported by other students, refined this delicate, trussed load-bearing structure. The path led from a structural and design idea through detail design to the production of the workshop space. I had the opportunity to accompany and supervise this experimental project from a constructional and artisanal perspective.

Transformation of the structural idea
into a comprehensive design

For the task of translating the load-bearing structure into an overarching idea, the following priorities were very important:

— Understand the basic principle and design rules of the load-bearing structure

— Find solutions within the design that strengthen the underlying idea
  — Win over teams from the other structural design groups for this new idea

Detail design

For the detail design, about ten students worked in roughly five groups of two and were given subtasks from the project as a whole. This resulted in the following topics and learning effects with many new and experimental priorities:
  — Designing and detailing with the raw material wood
  — Fitting together the various details from the planning groups into a whole (bring about a collective team decision)
  — Designing and detailing on the basis of the underlying idea
  — Designing and detailing to suit the production and materials
  — Producing construction models of the details

Production

The main load-bearing structure was produced by the students at our business premises with spontaneous support from the management team and skilled personnel from our production workforce. In this phase, it was possible to learn and develop many aspects:
  — Are the details also feasible to build?
  — Train one's understanding of handcraft
  — Develop and try out one's own production ideas
  — Coordination of specialists with different talents

Assembly

Assembly is the most specialised phase for every craftsperson and so too for the students. There is uncertainty about whether what has been produced will actually fit and can be joined together. The team experiences with its own senses whether what has been designed and engineered can also be produced and assembled. The students can also ask themselves whether the picture they have mentally conceived corresponds to the real picture. Added to that is the feeling of the joy of creation. The delight and the impact grow even stronger when the entire process is in the hands of the students.

In terms of construction and structural design, we have created structures that could not simply be pulled out of thin air and that an engineer would probably never have thought of. Architecture students are trained more creatively and have the freedom to approach the task in an open-minded way. The lack of knowledge is good for coming up with new ideas.

In conclusion, I would like to congratulate the students and teachers for this very beautiful timber construction project. But most of all, the courage of Carmen and Urs cannot be appreciated sufficiently. They had the courage to embark on the experiment and to travel the path with the students, from the structural idea to the finished building. In summary, it can be said that for everyone involved — that is, for the students, for the project team and for me — this is the best solution: learning by designing, detailing and engineering with wood.

123 Zeichnerische Reflexion Reflection in drawings

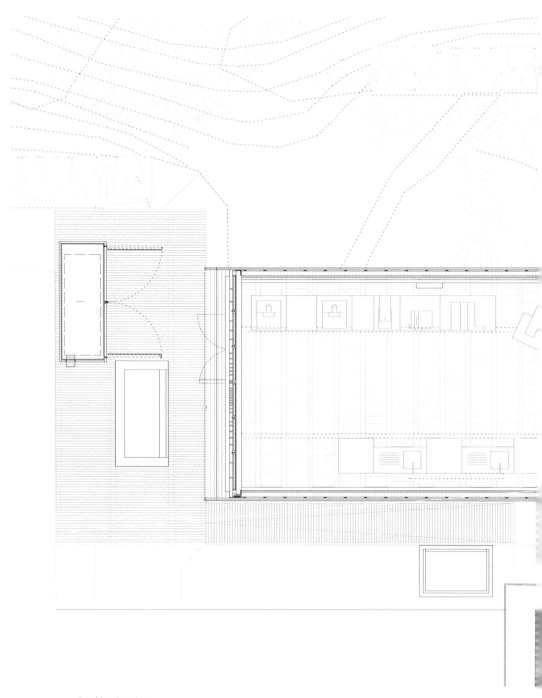

Grundriss Floor plan

Ausführungspläne Construction drawings

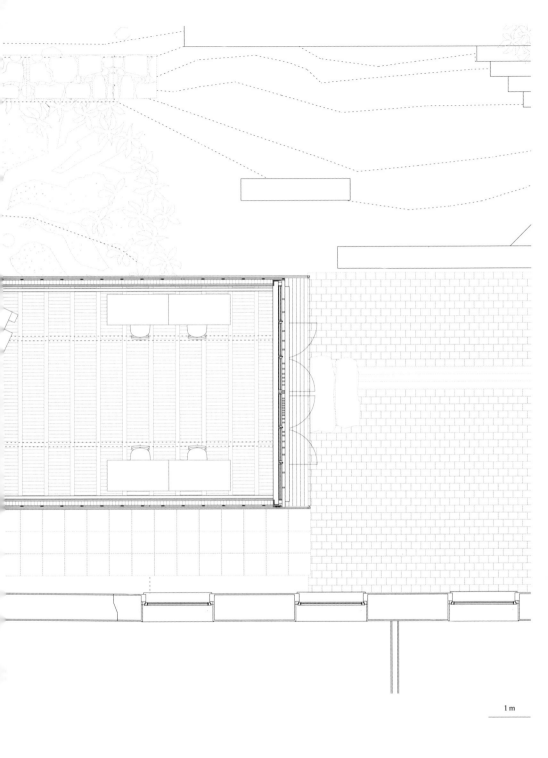

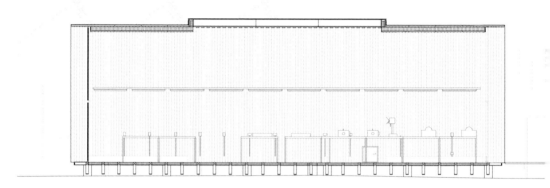

Längsschnitt Longitudinal section

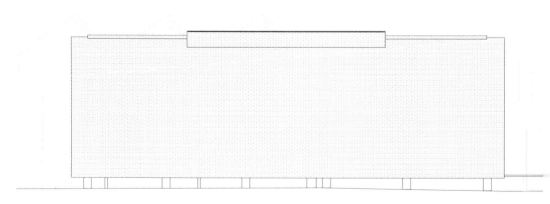

Längsansicht Longitudinal elevation

Ausführungspläne Construction drawings

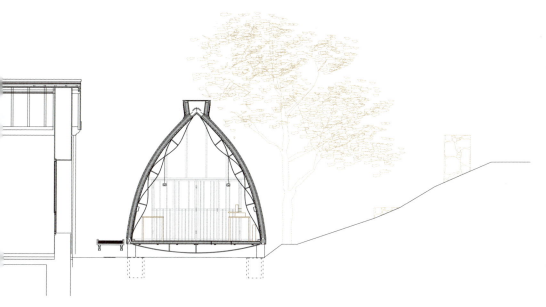

Querschnitt Cross section

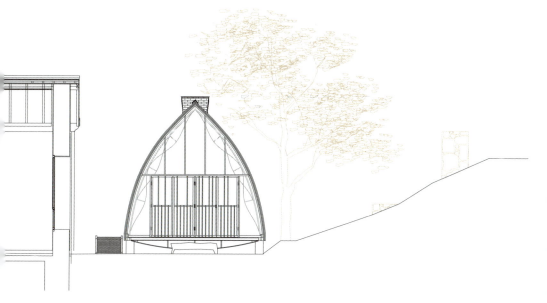

Frontansicht Elevation front

127

Es ging hier nicht nur um schöne Pläne und um eine gute Präsentation. Das Bauen ermöglichte ein breites Verständnis, war haptisch und weiterführend für die Architektur. Es bereichert definitiv jeden, der etwas im Massstab 1:1 umsetzt.

Kerstin Thurnher
BSc Studierende

This was not just about beautiful drawings and a good presentation. The act of building afforded a broad understanding; it was haptic and brought the architecture further. It is definitely enriching for anyone to implement something at a scale of 1:1.

Kerstin Thurnher
BSc student

Eröffnung Opening

Eröffnung Opening

Eröffnung Opening

Factbox
Fact Box

Zeitraum	Oktober 2016 – September 2017
Ort	Vaduz, Liechtenstein
Bauherrin	Universität Liechtenstein, Institut für Architektur und Raumentwicklung
Partner	Frommelt Zimmerei und Ing. Holzbau AG, Schaan, Liechtenstein
Holzherkunft, Zertifizierung Holz	Lokales Fichtenholz (LI), Lärchenschindeln aus dem Allgäu (DE)
Realisierung	Studierende in Kooperation mit der Frommelt Zimmerei und Ing. Holzbau AG, Schaan, Liechtenstein
Nachhaltigkeitskette	Entwurfsarbeit und Ausführung mit Studierenden sowie lokalen Zimmerleuten und weiteren Handwerkern

Technische Beschreibung

Tragkonstruktion	Holzlamellenbaustruktur, gedämmt 320 Holzlamellen à 5 Meter erzeugen in gebogenem Zustand durch ihre Spannung die Trag- und Grundkonstruktion
Heizungssystem	Holzpellet-Einzelofen
U-Werte Wand und Dach	0,17 W/m²K
Geschossanzahl	1
Geschossfläche	72 m²

Workshop Erasmus+ Crafting Wood 2016

Universität Liechtenstein, Vaduz

Dozierende
Urs Meister, Carmen Rist-Stadelmann, Christoph Frommelt
Studierende
Philipp Wilhelm Althammer, Christoph Ammer, Julia Beck,
Pascale Büchel, Christoph Fessler, Julia Forrer, Livia Audrey Herle,
Daniela Huber, Julia Mair, Lino Nägele, Anne-Lea Pfistner,
Denise Pfleger, Michelle Rheinberger, Simon Westreicher

Academie van Bouwkunst, Amsterdam

Dozierende
Machiel Spaan, Wouter Kroeze
Studierende
Alexander Beeloo, Midas van Boekel, Laurence de Kort, Salaheddine
Chekh Ibrahim, Kristina Kosic, Stefan Koster, Roxana Vakil Mozafari,
Dirk Overduin, Eldrich Piqué, Eva Souren, Paulien van der Valk,
Wouter van der Velpen, Joeri Verhoeven, Tristen Vreugdenhil

Mackintosh School of Architecture, Glasgow

Dozierende
Kathy Li, Anna Poston
Studierende
Fredrik Frendin, Mate Gehberger, Ewan Hepburn, Annie Higham,
Rebecca Hodolava, William McRoberts, Angus Riddell, Siripat Rojnirun,
Nichole Samson, Pavandip Sian, Ingrid Wennemo, Martin Zizka

Realisierung 2017

Universität Liechtenstein, Vaduz

Dozierende
Carmen Rist-Stadelmann, Urs Meister, Christoph Frommelt, Bianca Böckle

Studierende Studio Rist-Stadelmann, SS 2017
Pia Rebekka Alge, Manuel Bayer, Seraina Bernegger, Petra Bolter-Allgäuer, Andreas Brandstetter, Susanne Cäcilia Brandt, Selina Maria Capol, Ahmet Ciftcioglu, Angela Cosentino, Rocco Cutieri, Ruben De Sá, Eda Demir, Alexander Düringer, Simon Johannes Egger, Miriam Ender, David Elias Fetz, Jakob Fliri, Elena Florineth, Andrea Elisabeth Freund, Stephanie Beatrice Ganahl, Sandeep Gill, Miriam Gohm, Merve Hancer, Lennon Lee Hartmann, Martin Herwelly, Juliana Stefanie Hasler, Florian Heeb, Chiara Maria Jug, Eslem Karakoc, Serena Keller, David Kerle, Claudia Kuster, Sören Landinger, Natalie Marinelli, Christoph Müller, Gebhard Rudolf Natter, Ellena Chiara Joanna Neff, Nina Maria Oksakowski, Oscar Eduardo Sauseng, Sarah Juliana Schädler, Lara Anina Schmid, Nadine Schneider, Romana Schwitter, Emilie Stecher, Sara Manuela Thöny, Joanne Tschenett, Stefan Verling, Aurelia Louise Winter, Marcella Zauner, Maximilian Wilhelm Zwickl

Studierende Studio Meister, SS 2017
Philipp Wilhelm Althammer, Christoph Ammer, Viviane Elisabeth Göbel, Livia Audrey Herle, Alexander Peter Meissner, Lino Oliver Konrad Nägele, Albert Paletta, Dionys Rieder, Fabio Michael Schober, Kerstin Ulrike Thurnher

Zimmerei Frommelt und Ing. Holzbau AG
Pascal Benzer, David Eberle, Martin Lorez, Viktor Seethaler, Christoph Willinger

Time period	October 2016 – September 2017
Location	Vaduz, Liechtenstein
Client	University of Liechtenstein, Institute of Architecture and Planning
Partner	Frommelt Zimmerei und Ing. Holzbau AG, Schaan, Liechtenstein
Wood's origin and certification	Local spruce wood (LI), larch shingles from the Allgäu (DE)
Implementation	Students, in collaboration with Frommelt Zimmerei und Ing. Holzbau AG, Schaan, Liechtenstein
Sustainability chain	Design work and execution with students as well as local carpenters and other craftspeople

Technical description

Load-bearing structure	Wooden slat structure, insulated 320 wooden slats, each five metres long, form the load-bearing structure and main framework through the tension exerted in their bent state
Heating system	Wood pellet stove
U-values for wall and roof	0.17 W/m^{2}K
Number of floors	1
Floor area	72 m^2

Workshop Erasmus+ Crafting Wood 2016

University of Liechtenstein, Vaduz

Lecturers
Urs Meister, Carmen Rist-Stadelmann, Christoph Frommelt
Students
Philipp Wilhelm Althammer, Christoph Ammer, Julia Beck,
Pascale Büchel, Christoph Fessler, Julia Forrer, Livia Audrey Herle,
Daniela Huber, Julia Mair, Lino Nägele, Anne-Lea Pfistner,
Denise Pfleger, Michelle Rheinberger, Simon Westreicher

Academie van Bouwkunst, Amsterdam

Lecturers
Machiel Spaan, Wouter Kroeze
Students
Alexander Beeloo, Midas van Boekel, Laurence de Kort, Salaheddine
Chekh Ibrahim, Kristina Kosic, Stefan Koster, Roxana Vakil Mozafari,
Dirk Overduin, Eldrich Piqué, Eva Souren, Paulien van der Valk,
Wouter van der Velpen, Joeri Verhoeven, Tristen Vreugdenhil

Mackintosh School of Architecture, Glasgow

Lecturers
Kathy Li, Anna Poston
Students
Fredrik Frendin, Mate Gehberger, Ewan Hepburn, Annie Higham,
Rebecca Hodolava, William McRoberts, Angus Riddell, Siripat Rojnirun,
Nichole Samson, Pavandip Sian, Ingrid Wennemo, Martin Zizka

Realisation 2017

University of Liechtenstein, Vaduz

Lecturers
Carmen Rist-Stadelmann, Urs Meister, Christoph Frommelt, Bianca Böckle

Students Studio Rist-Stadelmann, SS 2017
Pia Rebekka Alge, Manuel Bayer, Seraina Bernegger, Petra Bolter-Allgäuer, Andreas Brandstetter, Susanne Cäcilia Brandt, Selina Maria Capol, Ahmet Ciftcioglu, Angela Cosentino, Rocco Cutieri, Ruben De Sá, Eda Demir, Alexander Düringer, Simon Johannes Egger, Miriam Ender, David Elias Fetz, Jakob Fliri, Elena Florineth, Andrea Elisabeth Freund, Stephanie Beatrice Ganahl, Sandeep Gill, Miriam Gohm, Merve Hancer, Lennon Lee Hartmann, Martin Herwelly, Juliana Stefanie Hasler, Florian Heeb, Chiara Maria Jug, Eslem Karakoc, Serena Keller, David Kerle, Claudia Kuster, Sören Landinger, Natalie Marinelli, Christoph Müller, Gebhard Rudolf Natter, Ellena Chiara Joanna Neff, Nina Maria Oksakowski, Oscar Eduardo Sauseng, Sarah Juliana Schädler, Lara Anina Schmid, Nadine Schneider, Romana Schwitter, Emilie Stecher, Sara Manuela Thöny, Joanne Tschenett, Stefan Verling, Aurelia Louise Winter, Marcella Zauner, Maximilian Wilhelm Zwickl

Students Studio Meister, SS 2017
Philipp Wilhelm Althammer, Christoph Ammer, Viviane Elisabeth Göbel, Livia Audrey Herle, Alexander Peter Meissner, Lino Oliver Konrad Nägele, Albert Paletta, Dionys Rieder, Fabio Michael Schober, Kerstin Ulrike Thurnher

Frommelt Zimmerei und Ing. Holzbau AG
Pascal Benzer, David Eberle, Martin Lorez, Viktor Seethaler, Christoph Willinger

Hands-on als didaktische Methode
(S. 22–26)

1. Revans, R. W. (2011). ABC of action learning. Gower, XIII.
2. Vgl. Dewey, J. (1938). Experience and Education. Kappa Delta Pi lecture series. Free Press, S. 51–60.
3. Vgl. ebd., S. 89.
4. Vgl. ebd., S. 70–71.
5. Vgl. ebd., S. 64.
6. Vgl. ebd., S. 19.
7. Vgl. ebd., S. 58.
8. Vgl. Kolb, D. A. (2014). Experiential learning: Experience as the source of learning and development / David A. Kolb (Second edition). Pearson Education Inc, S. 5.
9. Vgl.: Altrichter, H. (1990). Ist das noch wissenschaft? Darstellung und wissenschaftstheoretische diskussion einer von lehrern betriebenen aktionsforschung. Bildung-arbeit-gesellschaft: Bd. 3. Profil, S. 43–44.
10. Vgl. Lück, H. E. (2011). Anfänge der Wirtschaftspsychologie bei Kurt Lewin. Gestalt Theory, 33(2), S. 91–114, 106.
11. Vgl. Hart, E. & Felden, K. (2001). Aktionsforschung: Handbuch für Pflege-, Gesundheits- und Sozialberufe. Hans Huber Programmbereich Pflege. H. Huber, S. 24.
12. Vgl. Lewin, K. (1946). Action research and minority problems. Journal of Social issues, 2, S. 34–46.
13. Vgl. Hart, E. & Felden, K. (2001). Aktionsforschung: Handbuch für Pflege-, Gesundheits- und Sozialberufe. Hans Huber Programmbereich Pflege. H. Huber, S. 26–27.
14. Hart, E. & Felden, K. (2001). Aktionsforschung: Handbuch für Pflege-, Gesundheits- und Sozialberufe. Hans Huber Programmbereich Pflege. H. Huber, S. 27.
15. Vgl. Kolb, D. A. (2014). Experiential learning: Experience as the source of learning and development / David A. Kolb (Second edition). Pearson Education Inc, S. 34.
16. Vgl. Piaget, J. (1991). Das Erwachen der Intelligenz beim Kinde (3. Aufl.). Gesammelte Werke: Bd. 1. Klett, S. 163–180.
17. Vgl. Piaget, J. (1991). Das Erwachen der Intelligenz beim Kinde (3. Aufl.). Gesammelte Werke: Bd. 1. Klett, S. 180–191.
18. Vgl. Piaget, J. (1999). Über Pädagogik. Beltz-Taschenbuch: 1. Essay. Beltz, S. 23–27.
19. Wick, R. K. (1994). Bauhaus-Pädagogik (4. Aufl.). DuMont-Dokumente. DuMont, S. 158.
20. Albers, J. (1928). Werklicher Formunterricht. Bauhaus Zeitschrift, S. 2–7, 4.

Materialbewusstsein und Tektonik
(S. 37–41)

1. Kollhoff, H. (1993). Über Tektonik in der Baukunst. Vieweg, S. 7.
2. Vgl. Semper, G. (2012, reprint 1879). Der Stil in den technischen und tektonischen Künsten (Bd. 2). Nabu Public Domain Reprints, S. 199.
3. Loos, A. (2010). Gesammelte Schriften. Das Princip der Bekleidung (A. Opel, Hg.). Lesethek Verlag, S. 140.
4. Ebd., S. 141.
5. Loos, A. (2010). Gesammelte Schriften. Das Princip der Bekleidung (A. Opel, Hg.). Lesethek Verlag, S. 139.
6. Vgl. Sennett, R. (2008). Handwerk: Aus dem Amerikanischen von Michael Bischoff (2. Auflage). Verlag die Wirtschaft, S. 162–164.
7. Vgl. ebd., S. 164–176.
8. Vgl. ebd., S. 177–184.
9. Vgl. ebd., S. 184–196.
10. Pallasmaa, J. (2009). The thinking hand: Existential and embodied wisdom in architecture / Juhani Pallasmaa. AD primers. Wiley; Chichester: John Wiley [distributor], S. 82.
11. Vgl. Moholy-Nagy, L., Wingler, H. M. & Stelzer, O. (2001). Von Material zu Architektur (2. Aufl.). Neue Bauhausbücher. neue Folge der von Walter Gropius und Laszlo Moholy-Nagy begründeten „Bauhausbücher". Gebr. Mann Verlag, S. 21–29.
12. Horowitz, F. A. & Danilowitz, B. (2006). Josef Albers: To open eyes: the Bauhaus, Black Mountain College, and Yale / Frederick A. Horowitz and Brenda Danilowitz. Phaidon, S. 94.

Handwerk als kollektiver Prozess
(S. 52–56)

1. Kolb, D. A. (2014). Experiential learning: Experience as the source of learning and development / David A. Kolb (Second edition). Pearson Education Inc, S. 37.
2. Vgl. Pye, D. (1979). The nature and art of workmanship (2. tr., 1979). Cambridge Univ. Press, S. 11–12.
3. Vgl. Pevsner, N. (1966). Fünfhundert Jahre Künstlerausbildung. Fünfhundert Jahre Künstlerausbildung (H. M. Wingler, Hg.). Staatliche Kunstakademie Düsseldorf, Bauhaus-Archiv Darmstadt, S. 12.
4. Vgl. Lux, J. A. (2018, reprint 1908). Das neue Kunstgewerbe in Deutschland. Intank Publishing, S. 123.
5. Vgl. Bothe, R. & Wingler, H. M. (1977). Kunstschulreform 1900–1933. Gebr. Mann Studio-Reihe. Mann, S. 37.
6. Vgl. Semper, G. (1966). Wissenschaft, Industrie und Kunst. Neue Bauhausbücher. Florian Kupferberg Verlag, S. 47–49.
7. Vgl. Bothe, R. & Wingler, H. M. (1977). Kunstschulreform 1900–1933. Gebr. Mann Studio-Reihe. Mann, S. 39.
8. Vgl. Bothe, R. & Wingler, H. M. (1977). Kunstschulreform 1900–1933. Gebr. Mann Studio-Reihe. Mann, S. 39–40.
9. Vgl. Lux, J. A. (2018, reprint 1908). Das neue Kunstgewerbe in Deutschland. Intank Publishing, S. 51–55.
10. Vgl. Pevsner, N. (1966). Fünfhundert Jahre Künstlerausbildung. Fünfhundert Jahre Künstlerausbildung (H. M. Wingler, Hg.). Staatliche Kunstakademie Düsseldorf, Bauhaus-Archiv Darmstadt, S. 12–13.
11. Vgl. Tschepkunowa, I. (2015). WChUTEMAS – ein russisches Labor der Moderne: Architekturentwürfe 1920–1930; [anlässlich der Ausstellung WChUTEMAS im Martin-Gropius-Bau Berlin, 5. Dezember 2014 – 6. April 2015]. Berliner Festspiele.
12. Vgl. Bothe, R. & Wingler, H. M. (1977). Kunstschulreform 1900–1933. Gebr. Mann Studio-Reihe. Mann, S. 41.

Methoden des Bauens
(S. 67–72)

1. Buckminster, F. (12. November 1966). How little I know. Saturday Review, S. 29–31, 31.
2. Vgl. Moholy-Nagy, L., Wingler, H. M. & Stelzer, O. (2001). Von Material zu Architektur (2. Aufl.). Neue Bauhausbücher. neue Folge der von Walter Gropius und Laszlo Moholy-Nagy begründeten „Bauhausbücher". Gebr. Mann Verlag, S. 10–11.
3. Vgl. Pallasmaa, J. (2009). The thinking hand: Existential and embodied wisdom in architecture / Juhani Pallasmaa. AD primers. Wiley; Chichester: John Wiley [distributor], S. 65.
4. Vgl. Wick, R. K. (1994). Bauhaus-Pädagogik (4. Aufl.). DuMont-Dokumente. DuMont, S. 64.
5. Vgl. Locke, J. & Wohlers, H. (2007). Gedanken über Erziehung. Reclams Universal-Bibliothek Nr. 6147. Reclam, S. 253–257.
6. Vgl. Arendt, H. (2018). Vita activa oder Vom tätigen Leben (19. Aufl.). Piper: Bd. 3623. Piper, S. 119.
7. Vgl. Rousseau, J.-J. & Charrak, A. (2009). Émile, ou, De l'éducation. GF: Bd. 1428. Flammarion.
8. Vgl. Russ, W. (1973). Geschichte der Pädagogik (9. Aufl.). Klinkhardts pädagogische Abrisse. Klinkhardt, S. 63–69.
9. Vgl. ebd., S. 93–101.
10. Vgl. ebd., S. 104–107.
11. Oswalt, P. (Hg.). (2019). Bauwelt Fundamente: Bd. 164. Hannes Meyers neue Bauhauslehre: Von Dessau nach Mexiko. Birkhäuser, S. 141.
12. Vrachliotis, G. (2018, Dezember). Architekturmaschine. Arch+, 51. Jahrgang, S. 36–42, 37.

Hands-on Didactics
(pp. 27–31)

Revans, R. W. (2011). *ABC of Action Learning*. Gower, xiii.
Dewey, J. (1938). *Experience and Education*. Kappa Delta Pi lecture series. Free Press, 51–60.
Dewey, J. (1938), 89.
Dewey, J. (1938), 70–71.
Dewey, J. (1938), 64.
Dewey, J. (1938), 19.
Dewey, J. (1938), 58.
Kolb, D. A. (2014). *Experiential Learning: Experience as the Source of Learning and Development*, 2nd ed. Pearson Education, 5.
Altrichter, H. (1990). *Ist das noch Wissenschaft? Darstellung und wissenschaftstheoretische Diskussion einer von lehrern betriebenen aktionsforschung*. Bildung, Arbeit, Gesellschaft, vol. 3. Profil, 43–44.
Lück, H. E. (2011). 'Anfänge der Wirtschaftspsychologie bei Kurt Lewin'. *Gestalt Theory* 33(2), 91–114, 106.
Hart, E. / Bond, M. (2001). *Aktionsforschung: Handbuch für Pflege-, Gesundheits- und Sozialberufe*, trans. K. Felden. Hans Huber, 24. Originally published as *Action Research For Health And Social Care: A Guide to Practice* (McGraw-Hill, 1995).
Lewin, K. (1946). 'Action Research and Minority Problems'. *Journal of Social Issues* 2, 34–46.
Hart, E. / Bond, M. (2001), 26–27.
Hart, E. / Bond, M. (2001), 27.
Kolb, D. A. (2014), 34.
Piaget, J. (1991). *Das Erwachen der Intelligenz beim Kinde*, 3rd ed., trans. B. Seiler. Klett, 163–180. Originally published in 1936 as *La naissance de l'intelligence chez l'enfant*; translated into English as *The Origins of Intelligence in Children*.
Piaget, J. (1991), 180–191.
Piaget, J. (1999). *Über Pädagogik*, trans. I. Kuhn / R. Stamm. Beltz, 23–27. Anthology, originally published in 1998 as *De la pédagogie*.
Wick, R. K. (1994). *Bauhaus-Pädagogik*, 4th ed. DuMont, 158.
Albers, J. (1928). 'Werklicher Formunterricht'. *Bauhaus Zeitschrift* 2 (⅔), 3–7, 4. Translated into English as 'Teaching Form Through Practice', albersfoundation.org/teaching/josef-albers/texts/# (accessed 25 Mar. 2021).

Material Consciousness and Tectonics
(pp. 42–46)

Kollhoff, H. (1993). *Über Tektonik in der Baukunst*. Vieweg, 7.
Semper, G. (2012). *Der Stil in den technischen und tektonischen Künsten*, vol. 2, reprint of 1879 ed. Nabu Public Domain Reprints, 199. Translated into English as *Style in the Technical and Tectonic Arts* (Getty, 2004).
Loos, A. (2010). *Gesammelte Schriften. Das Princip der Bekleidung*, ed. A. Opel. Lesethek Verlag, 140.
Loos, A. (2010), 141.
Loos, A. (2010), 139.
Sennett, R. (2008). *Handwerk*, trans. M. Bischoff, 2nd ed. Verlag die Wirtschaft, 162–164. Originally published as *The Craftsman* (Yale, 2008).
Sennett, R. (2008), 164–176.
Sennett, R. (2008), 177–184.
Sennett, R. (2008), 184–196.
Pallasmaa, J. (2009). *The Thinking Hand: Existential and Embodied Wisdom in Architecture*. AD Primers. Wiley, 82.

11 Moholy-Nagy, L. / Wingler, H. M. / Stelzer, O. (2001). *Von Material zu Architektur*, reprint of 1929 orig. ed. 'Neue Bauhausbücher'. New installment of the Bauhaus Books series founded by Walter Gropius and Laszlo Moholy-Nagy. Gebr. Mann Verlag, 21–29.
12 Horowitz, F. A. / Danilowitz, B. (2006). *Josef Albers: To Open Eyes—The Bauhaus, Black Mountain College, and Yale*. Phaidon, 94.

Craft as a Collective Process
(pp. 57–61)

1 Kolb, D. A. (2014). *Experiential Learning: Experience as the Source of Learning and Development*, 2nd ed. Pearson Education, 37.
2 Pye, D. (1978). *The Nature and Art of Workmanship*, reprint of orig. 1968 ed. Cambridge Univ. Press, 11–12.
3 Pevsner, N. (1966). *Fünfhundert Jahre Künstlerausbildung: William Morris—2 Vorträge*. Staatliche Kunstakademie Düsseldorf, Bauhaus-Archiv Darmstadt, 12.
4 Lux, J. A. (2018). *Das neue Kunstgewerbe in Deutschland*, reprint of orig. 1908 ed. Intank, 123.
5 Bothe, R. / Wingler, H. M. (1977). *Kunstschulreform 1900–1933*. Gebr. Mann, 37.
6 Semper, G. (1966). *Wissenschaft, Industrie und Kunst*, orig. pub. 1852. Neue Bauhausbücher. Florian Kupferberg Verlag, 47–49.
7 Bothe, R. / Wingler, H. M. (1977), 39.
8 Bothe, R. / Wingler, H. M. (1977), 39–40.
9 Lux, J. A. (2018), 51–55.
10 Pevsner, N. (1966), 12–13.
11 Tschepkunowa [Chepkunova], I. (2015). *WChUTEMAS: Ein russisches Labor der Moderne—Architekturentwürfe 1920–1930*. Catalogue accompanying the exhibition at Martin-Gropius-Bau Berlin, 5 December 2014–6 April 2015. Berliner Festspiele.
12 Bothe, R. / Wingler, H. M. (1977), 41.

Methods of Building
(pp. 73–78)

1 Fuller, R. Buckminster (1966). 'How Little I Know'. *Saturday Review*, 12 November 1966, 29–31, 31.
2 Moholy-Nagy, L. / Wingler, H. M. / Stelzer, O. (2001). *Von Material zu Architektur*, reprint of 1929 orig. ed. Neue Bauhausbücher. New installment of the Bauhaus Books series founded by Walter Gropius and Laszlo Moholy-Nagy. Gebr. Mann Verlag, 10–11.
3 Pallasmaa, J. (2009). *The Thinking Hand: Existential and Embodied Wisdom in Architecture*. AD Primers. Wiley, 65.
4 Wick, R. K. (1994). *Bauhaus-Pädagogik*, 4th ed. DuMont, 64.
5 Locke, J. / Wohlers, H. (2007). *Gedanken über Erziehung*. Reclams Universal-Bibliothek no. 6147. Reclam, 253–257.
6 Arendt, H. (2018). *Vita activa oder Vom tätigen Leben*, 19th ed. Piper no. 3623. Piper, 119. Originally published as *The Human Condition* (Univ. of Chicago Press, 1958).
7 Rousseau, J.-J. / Charrak, A. (2009). *Émile, ou, De l'éducation*. GF no. 1428. Éditions Flammarion. Originally published in 1762; translated into English as *Emile, or On Education*.
8 Russ, W. (1973). *Geschichte der Pädagogik*, 9th printing. Klinkhardts pädagogische Abrisse. Klinkhardt, 63–69.
9 Russ, W. (1973), 93–101.

10 Russ, W. (1973), 104–107.
11 Oswalt, P., ed. (2019). *Hannes Meyers neue Bauhauslehre: Von Dessau nach Mexiko*. Bauwelt Fundamente 164. Birkhäuser, 141.
12 Vrachliotis, G. (2018). *Architekturmaschine*. Arch+ 234, 36–43, 37.

Herausgeber Editors
Carmen Rist-Stadelmann, Urs Meister

Textbeiträge Contributions
Carmen Rist-Stadelmann, Urs Meister,
Machiel Spaan, Christoph Frommelt

Übersetzung Translation
David Koralek, Billy Nolan

Korrektorat Englisch Proofreading English
David Koralek / ArchiTrans

Korrektorat Deutsch Proofreading German
Sabine Bockmühl

Grafik Design
SJG / Joost Grootens, Dimitri Jeannottat

Lithografie Image processing
Marjeta Morinc

Druck und Bindung Printing and binding
Wilco Art Books
Gedruckt in den Niederlanden / Printed in the Netherlands

© 2022 die Autoren / the authors und / and Park Books AG, Zürich

Park Books
Niederdorfstrasse 54
8001 Zürich
Schweiz / Switzerland
www.park-books.com

ISBN 978-3-03860-236-1

Bildnachweis *Picure credits*
© Bruno Klomfar (Umschlag / Cover, 7L, 7R, 11R, 34, 47, 55, 59, 60L, 60R, 70R, 75L, 76L, 76R, 95R, 101L, 101R, 106L, 106R, 112, 113, 114–115, 145–160)
© Darko Todorovic (1, 69, 70L, 109, 110, 111, 129, 130, 131, 132)
Alle anderen Bilder, Pläne und Skizzen wurden von Studierenden und Dozierenden erstellt
All other pictures, drawings and sketches by students and teachers

Spezieller Dank an *Special thanks to*
Universität Liechtenstein, Vaduz
Frommelt Zimmerei Ing. Holzbau AG, Schaan
Gemeinde Schaan, Liechtenstein
Agentur für Internationale Bildungsangelegenheiten, Vaduz

Park Books wird vom Bundesamt für Kultur mit einem Strukturbeitrag für die Jahre 2021–2024 unterstützt.
Park Books is being supported by the Federal Office of Culture with a general subsidy for the years 2021–2024.

Alle Rechte vorbehalten; kein Teil dieser Publikation darf ohne vorherige schriftliche Zustimmung des Herausgebers in irgendeiner Form oder mit irgendwelchen Mitteln — elektronisch, mechanisch, durch Fotokopie, Aufzeichnung oder auf andere Weise — vervielfältigt, in gespeichert oder übertragen werden.
All rights reserved; no part of this publication may be reproduced, stored in a retrieval system or transmitted in any form or by any means — electronic, mechanical, photocopying, recording or otherwise — without the prior written consent of the publisher.

Dieses Projekt wurde mit Unterstützung der Europäischen Kommission finanziert. Die Verantwortung für den Inhalt dieser Veröffentlichung trägt allein der Verfasser; die Kommission haftet nicht für die weitere Verwendung der darin enthaltenen Angaben.
This project has been funded with support from the European Commission. This publication reflects the views only of the author, and the Commission cannot be held responsible for any use which may be made of the information contained therein.